“Diary of a Hundred Years” Or “What Happened in Birstall Between 1900 and 2000”

Random jottings of the 20th Century

by John Kilby

Foreword

My grandson, Christopher wondered if I could mention him in these recollections. So, Christopher Edward Kilby, have a look at the entry for 1989.

Christopher Edward Kilby		1989
Richard William Kilby		1961
John Arthur Kilby		1932
Arthur Lewis Kilby		1898
Arthur Kilby		1866
William Kilby		1835
Robert Kilby		1805
Thomas Kilby		1780
Robert Kilby		1751
Robert Kilby		1720
Thomas Kilby		????
Thomas Kilby	died	1707

You will find me, John Arthur Kilby, third in line of descent, just above Arthur Lewis Kilby who is my father and Christopher's great grandfather. For many years my grandfather, Arthur Kilby, was head gardener at Birstall Hall and the life span of my grandfather, my father and myself has encompassed the whole of the twentieth century. Between us we have witnessed, or were aware of, most of the events and personalities recorded in this diary of Birstall of the 1900's. The above then, is the list of male descendants all of whom were born in Birstall, or whose parents lived in the village at the time of their birth.

It is to my father, our three children, our seven grandchildren and all the other Kilby's past and present that I dedicate this village memoir.

Acknowledgements

I would like to thank the following Birstall citizens past and present for their memories and detailed reminiscences on the following village topics.

David Bass, Women's Land Army.
John Charles, Greengate Lane Homesteads.
Edna Chester, Women's Land Army.
Joyce Forder, Women's Land Army.
Geoffrey Gibson, Birstall Telephone Exchange, St James Church.
Beryl Kilby, my sister.
Dorothy Riley, Women's Land Army.
Shirley Scott, Wanlip Hall.
Maisie Slater (nee Walton), Lawn Cinema.
Mike Smith, Photographs and historical miscellanea.
Chris Timmis, her father, Snap Green.

Other organisations who have assisted me in compiling these records.
Birstall Parish Council, The Leicester Mercury, Leicester Journals.

Other persons outside the village who have also helped.
Tom and Margaret Shaw of Wigston, for their notes and photographs of the Kemp and Shaw buses.

Special thanks to Stuart Liquorish for scanning and setting the photographs and to Betty and Mike Smith for proof reading this diary at least twice.

Finally, I would record my thanks to my wife Rosalie, for all her patience and endurance, when night after night I was sitting in front of the word processor typing these memories.

1900 - 1909

1900 The celebrations to herald the new century were marred by events in South Africa. Birstall had an important involvement in that Lt. Arthur Crisp Clarke, the son of Joseph Crisp Clarke, village Squire, who lived at Birstall Hall, was serving his country in the Boer War in the South Africa. He was in the Argyll and Sutherland Highlanders and his return in 1903 was quite triumphant. The villagers of Birstall, together with the staff of the Hall, went down to Belgrave to meet the horse and trap. The horses were removed and the decorated trap was pulled over the new bridge and up Red Hill. (This bridge was still referred to, even in the middle of the nineteen hundreds as the 'New Bridge' although it had been built in 1822.) The Drive to the Hall was bedecked with bunting and signs of praise and thanksgiving for his safe return. Regrettably, his sister Evelyn Grace (Blakeway) had died during his absence at the tender age of 25 and her grave and memorial are sited just inside the entrance to the Church Yard, underneath the 'kneeling angel'.

1901 The population of the village at this time was 611, of which about 147 were Parliamentary electors.

January the 1st saw the River Soar burst its banks. It was nearly 7 feet above its normal level at the Aylestone Road Gasworks.

On the 22nd January Queen Victoria died and the accession of King Edward VII was proclaimed.

Miss Elizabeth While, the local benefactor, gave a parcel of land to the Parish Church in order that the churchyard burial ground could be extended. The sexton, John Smith, was quite pleased about this, as the parcel of land was very much higher than the roadway. This was due to the large amount of top-soil that had been deposited there at the time the canal and lock had been excavated in the later part of the 18th cent. The task of digging graves, from then onwards, became so much easier as the soil on this extended piece of land was less impacted. The Curate in charge at this time was the Rev. H. Parker.

Birstall Golf Club was founded and their first President was Mr Charles Bennion. He was also the founder of the British United Shoe Machinery Company, where a very large number of employees came from Birstall. Mr Bennion is probably best known for his generous bequest of Bradgate Park to the people of Leicestershire.

1902 The coronation of Edward VII took place on the 9th August. It had been postponed from the 26th June due to the King's illness with appendicitis and peritonitis.

1904 On the 21st April the first electric tram came along the extended line to Belgrave. The first regular horse drawn tram service to Belgrave had begun in 1874. A Toll Booth and shelter were provided at a point where today's entrance to Jelson's stands.

The first 'Daily Mirror' was published.

1906 An extension to the Reading Room was carried out. Mr William Henry Walker who had built 'The Holt' in 1871 and died there in 1903, together with the co-operation of other village gentry had, in 1876, built the Reading Room. A plaque in the front hall reads 'These rooms are a memorial to William Henry and Anne Jane Walker'. Over the past century these rooms have been put to many uses, Scout Hut, Gymnasium, Library, Meeting Room,

Dispensary and not least as an overflow classroom for the school. Alongside, and to the rear of the Reading Room, were some small dwellings known as Victoria Cottages.

Mr Walker, before building The Holt, had previously lived in the 15th century Cottage, at the bottom of School Lane, which is known by some, as 'The Chantry House'. The elaborate grounds boasted one of the first Alpine Gardens in Leicester and the water garden with its heathers, rhododendrons and azaleas, now located in the grounds of 'Holly Hayes', is still worth a visit. On vacating the Cottage for the new house, Mr Walker altered the deeds of the Cottage to ensure that the gardens were to be opened every year, in aid of charity.

1909 Lloyd George, as Chancellor of the Exchequer introduced the Old Age Pension on the 1st January.

The first crossing of the English Channel in an aeroplane, was made by Louis Bleriot on the 25th July.

1910 – 1919

1910 Mr John T Clarke, of Leicester, built the county's first radio transmitter and receiver on land in front of his holiday cottage at 91 Park Road. Earlier he had installed in his Leicester house a telephone to his workshop, believed to be the first private line in the town. The equipment at Park Road was housed at the top of a 40ft high tower, and consisted of a large coil of wire and a glass tube containing iron filings known as a coherer. There was a rubber mat at the top of the 40ft structure so that when the sparks flew people on the tower were less likely to get an electric shock from the metal grating. Later, a type of crystal detector was used instead of the coherer. It could receive signals from the Eiffel Tower and was in use until 1913 when Mr Clarke moved. It is interesting to note that at one time Park Road was to have been called 'Society Road'. I would subscribe to the notion that **Birstall Lighthouse** was in fact the Radio Transmitting Gallery in Park Road.

Dr Crippen, the notorious murderer, although not connected with Birstall, was executed in this year. There was however a Rothley man, Mr Wainwright, whose visits to the Harley Street surgery were interrupted by Dr Crippen being arrested on board the Atlantic Liner S S *Montrose,* by way of a radio call from the police in London. Apparently Dr Hawley Harvey Crippen had poisoned his wife, Cora, but said that she had gone to attend a sick relative in America. Then he said she had died there. Ethel le Neve, Dr. Crippen's mistress, moved into the house, which prompted the police to call and they found Mrs Crippen's mutilated corpse, covered in lime, in the cellar. Crippen and le Neve fled, and after a transatlantic chase and a radio message, they were arrested on arrival in New York. He was executed and le Neve was acquitted.

The Leicester Architect, Cecil Ogden, purchased the 'Coach House' (later to become 'The Clock House') from the Birstall Hall Estate. At the same time, the Head Gardener, Mr Arthur Kilby, my grandfather, who was acting as selling agent for the Joseph Crisp Clarke Estate, bought the 'Hall Cottage'. This was later to be known as 'The Old Cottage'. The stables, previously the home for six large hunters, the extensive vineries and part of the Hall gardens were also purchased to enable him to continue providing fresh fruit and vegetables to the people of Birstall. He had lived in 'Hall Cottage' since 1901 as Head Gardener and was able to purchase the tied cottage as a sitting tenant. A large parcel of land at the bottom of Roman Road, bordered by East Road, Perseverance Road and Freehold Road had already been sold to the East Leicester Land Society.

There were two carriers, in the village, plying for trade to take goods into Leicester or bring them back. One, Mr Toone went to 'The Coach and Horses' at 34 Humberstone Gate on Mondays, Wednesdays and Saturdays. The other, Mr Jack Wadd, went to and from the 'White Horse' at 27 Belgrave Gate, on Mondays, Wednesdays, Fridays and Saturdays.

It cost 1d. to post a letter, at this time, providing that it did not exceed 4ozs.

King Edward VII died on 6th May, and George V became King.

1911 There were only a few houses on the Birstall Hall estate and an excellent view of Leicester and the Soar valley could be obtained from the 'Slopes'. These are the large houses situated high up on the Birstall Road. During this year, St. George's Church in Leicester was burnt down and the fire could be clearly seen. It continued to burn for a week. When it was eventually rebuilt, the spire, that had previously adorned the building, was not replaced.

1912 National Telephone Company installed a telephone system for Birstall in 49 Front Street. Earlier in 1908 the village had a call office operated by Herbert Moulson and in 1912 by Mrs Louis Painter. In 1927 the Gibson family assumed responsibility for operating the system. The Gibson's were an established Birstall family who, before the First World War, lived at the Lodge to The Lawn where Fred Gibson was head gardener to Miss Partington. In 1916, whilst Mr Gibson was serving with the Royal Garrison Artillery, Miss Partington lost all her money, due to failing shares, and vacated The Lawn. Mrs Gibson had to move to Syston where she was employed as caretaker/operator of Syston telephone exchange until 1927. The Birstall exchange remained in the Gibson house at 49 Front Street from 1927 until 1938 when a new Automatic exchange was opened at the bottom of Johnson Road.

Here are some of Birstall's original phone numbers.

1	Thomas Worthington, Tempest Rd.
2	William Brockington, (later to be Sir William) 507 Loughborough Rd.
3	The Fielding Johnsons, Goscote Hall.
4	Dr Chappell, 5 Tempest Rd.
5	G W Innocent, Gwendolin Ave.
6	Birstall Station (LNER)
7	Mr G E Bouskell, Cliffe House.
8	Mr Newton, "The Pines"
9	The Exchange.
10	Mr L O Smith, "Clovelly" Park Rd.

11	The Boat House
12	
13	W F (Fred) B Smith, Church Hill.
14	Mr Richard Hallam, (later Alderman) 31 Tempest Rd.
15	Mr F Briers, The Lawn.
16	
17	Dr Mason The Drive (now 517 Lobro’ Rd.)
18	
19	Miss Johnson, “High Barn” The Slopes.
20	George Cook, 115 Roman Rd.
21	Mr Edwin Briggs, 24 Park Rd.
22	Mr W H Collett, 32 Park Rd.
23	Priestnall’s, “The Larches” Park Rd.
24	
25	
26	Ernest Wright, “The Grange”
27	Mrs Inglewood Clarke, 12 Tempest Rd.
28	W Fergusson, 1, Curzon Ave.
29	Miss Heard, “Hill Crest” 142 Birstall Rd.
30	H Hartshorn, Firfield Ave.
31	
32	W Beadle, Gravel Pits, Thurmaston.
33	J A V Boddy, Netherhall Farm.
34	Mr A Bates, “Guy Harlings” Birstall Rd.
35	
36	
37	Austin’s Newsagents (before Pearns)
38	
39	
40	
41	
42	
43	B U S M Co Sports Ground (Mr Hill)
44	G H Rudkin, “Skelwith” 31 Roman Rd.
45	Ald. Thos. Gooding, “The Poplars”

46 Thurmaston Police Station.
47
48 Mr and Mrs Letts, 74 Roman Rd.
49 Mr Charles Hoggett, 27 Tempest Rd.
50 Birstall Golf Club.
51 Mr A C Goadby, "Springfield" 33 Roman Rd.
52 Mr J C Vincent, "Pennard House" 40 Park Rd.
53
54 Mr I Bowler, "The Close" School Lane.
55 Mr Dukes-Farrell, 52 Park Rd.
56 Mr Richardson, Sibson Rd.
57 Petrol Station, Loughborough Rd.
58 Harriet Hincks, White Horse
59
60 Mr T H Bristow, 4 Park Rd.
61 Dr Larson, 621 Loughborough Rd.
62 Police House, 36 Greengate Lane.
63 Dr. Parker, 432 Loughborough Rd.
64 Robert Mackley, "Brightside" Park Rd.
65
66 Mr Cartwright, 84 Park Rd.
67 Mr and Mrs Spradbury, The Crossways.
74 Philip Stone (Chemist) Sibson Rd. (now Boots).
77 Mr Arthur Russell, 24 Tempest Rd.
81 Mr Archer, 168 Birstall Rd.
82 Orton's Coal Merchants 11 The Crossways.
83 Mr C E Hunt, "Delamere" 17 Tempest Rd.
84 The Misses Duxbury, 9 Curzon Ave.
85 Winterton's Grocers Sibson Rd. (Now Fresh Approach)
86 Leicestershire Co-op, The Crossways.
87 Mr S W Wilkinson, "Crowlands" 30 Park Rd.
88 Thomson Grocers, Sibson Rd.
89 Canon James and Miss Went, "The Cottage"
90 Birstall Vicarage.
91 Ernest Spiers, Park Rd.

92 W (Billy) Coates, Haulage Transport, Wanlip Ave.
93 Godfrey's Dyers, The Mill Church Hill.
94 Police, 51 Front St.
96 Geoffrey Wilkes, "Northlea" 29 Tempest Rd.
100 Mr William Cart, "Claremont House" Netherhall Lane.

1913 According to Albert Hunt, Birstall Mill, at the bottom of Church Hill was run by The Leicester Paper Staining Company. They were involved in the manufacture of leather board for the Motor Car industry, and eventually, the Mill was run by Godfreys the Dyers.

1914 An interesting article appeared in the Leicester Mercury in December this year. There was an account of the funeral of Joshua Palmer, who was an uncle of my grandmother.

Ex-Drayman's Funeral at Birstall
Fifty Years with the Midland Railway

The funeral took place at Birstall this afternoon of the late Joshua Palmer, a retired Midland Railway drayman, who was well known in Leicester and at one time was quite a character in the town. "Josh" as he was familiarly styled by his associates, was one of the tallest carters in the employ of the company, and in his younger days was very popular among his comrades. He had, however, one failing – being a little too fond of responding to the invitation to "have a glass." But he always did his work well, though at times he was indebted to the sagacity of his horse for a safe arrival at the depot.

Some 10 years ago, when Mr Arthur W Faire was with Sir Edward Wood in Wellington Street, he was attracted by "Josh" and after many friendly talks persuaded him to sign the pledge. This was the turning point in Palmer's life, and he, so rapidly improved his position that when the time came for his retirement from the service of the Midland Railway Company, he managed to save a rather substantial sum, which, invested in local industrial companies, brought him an income which, if not very large, enabled him to live in comfort during the closing days of

his life, which he spent in Birstall. How, Mr Faire's, good advice bore fruit was shown afterwards when the deceased was mainly instrumental in starting the Midland Railway Temperance Society – an organisation in which there are now many hundreds of members.
Palmer never forgot those whose advice had helped him into this position, and often called to see Mr Arthur Faire and Sir Samuel and Mr John E Faire, who had also taken a personal interest in his welfare.
'The interment of the body of Palmer was impressive, if only by reason of the lack of ostentation in the ceremony. The small party of mourners walked from the deceased's house, preceded by the flower-laden coffin, to the church, where the Rev. R B Disney (vicar of Belgrave and Birstall) conducted a service. Many of the deceased's friends, who knew him well and worked with him during his 50 years service with the Midland Railway Company – men who, to use words of one, thought "he ought to be buried in a marble grave, so good and charitable was he" – were present at the church. Sir Samuel Faire and Mr A W Faire attended, and there were also present: Messrs D.Gunby. F. Green. (Wigston). C. Harris, Elijah Kirk, J. L. Freer, W. Hallam, W. Woofenden, C. Joyce, and E. Buswell.
The coffin was of plain oak, with brass mountings, and bore the following inscription: "Joshua Palmer, died December 7th 1914, aged 75 years" Among the floral tributes was a beautiful wreath from Mr John E. Faire, Sir Samuel Faire and Mr Arthur W. Faire.

I am reminded of 'Uncle Josh' when I pass those beautiful Victorian premises of Faire Bros., in Rutland St. with the face of the building covered in marble cladding. In 1860 Joshua Palmer had been involved in carting Mountsorrel granite, from the barges moored at the canal wharf, against 'The White Horse', for the building of the New School premises and the relocation of the Blacksmiths Forge to Birstall Rd. He had lived at 41 Front St. with his older sisters.

1914 – 1918 The Great War Years

The 'Great War' 4th August 1914 to 11th November 1918 affected many people in Birstall and as many as 19 local men and boys lost their lives during the four year period. Mr and Mrs Thomas Fielding-Johnson, of Goscote Hall, were only one set of parents who lost a member of their family. Their son Henry Goode Fielding Johnson, had joined the army in July 1914 as a despatch rider but was tragically killed, at the Battle of Mons in France on the 23rd August in the same year. Henry had been sent with a message to 15 Brigade H. Q., he was never seen again. It was not until 1916 that he was officially posted 'Missing believed killed 23rd August 1914'. Most of the casualties of the war occurred during the battle of the Somme in July 1916. One Birstall soldier, 'Jimmy' wrote to my grandparents on the 20th September 1915. The letter is reproduced below:

13097
Gun Section
8thLeicesters
B.E.F. 20.9.15.

Dear Mr and Mrs Kilby,

Just a line to thank you very much for the nice parcel you sent to me. I was very sorry that the apricots didn't stand the journey, they got rather squashed but the cigarettes and cake were alright. The letter got a bit stained too but I was able to read it alright so far. I had just come out of the trenches when I got your parcel but now I am at a machine gun school for a few days doing a course of machine gun work. The weather is nice and fine and we were rather lucky we only had two light showers while we were in the trenches. We had a pretty good lot of shell-fire and some of 'Fritz's' aerial torpedoes and whiz-bangs. I expect we shall soon be going in again now. There are some rare sights here! Villages all smashed up. We are billeted in a Farmhouse and we have rigged it up quite nice. We have wire netting beds set about a foot and a half off the floor and we are surrounded by apple trees. All the people have left and the apples are lying all over the ground. We have'nt had many casualties yet – our worst happening was while they were practicing throwing bombs a few weeks ago.

Of course, there are many more things happening that I shall have to relate to you after it is all over – if I get through alright! We can't put anything in our letters as they have to be censored and if it gets in the enemies hands he learns more than is good for him. We are getting on very nicely so far and shall continue to while the weather keeps alright. I don't think I should much like to live in France – well not in this part anyway. It seems to be a hundred years behind times. It is all cornfields here and the villages are mostly made up of half mud houses. Well I hope you will be able to read this. It is dark and I am lying down to write.

I must close now with kind regards to you all.

I remain,

Yours Jimmie.

P S The light I am using to write by is a piece of flannelette in a tobacco tin.

This letter was from Sgt. James Reed who lived with his parents on Wanlip Lane. One of his sisters was Nellie Reed who became Mrs Hefford and much later on they lived at

23 Wanlip Lane next to where Somerfield is now. Unfortunately Jimmie died on the 15th July 1916 in that terrible 'Battle of the Somme', when there were about 420,000 British casualties. He and all the others are remembered annually on Remembrance Sunday. Jimmie's name also appears on the War Memorial at Bitteswell as he was employed, before the war in that village, as a groom to George Hodges Crisp Clarke, Arthur's elder brother by three years. George was a partner in his father's business and lived at the 'Elms' in Bitteswell and was Reed's employer. Jimmie was also a very popular member of the Birstall Village Football Team.

Major Jack Dakin who lived at 118 Roman Road, was awarded the highest Belgian honour in 1919. He was a Lt. In the 4th/5th Leicester's and won the 'Croix de Guerre'.

Mr and Mrs Arthur Kilby, my grandparents, received another letter from France at about the same time. This was from Lt. Col. Arthur Crisp Clarke, son of Joseph who had died in 1913, and although written on the 30th May 1915, did not arrive until the 26th November 1915. The contents of the letter are set out below.

Headquarters
27th Division
May 30th 1915

Dear Arthur,

I told you I would write and tell you how I got on – and I am lucky to be still here to do so. Anyway during the last 3 weeks I have taken part in what many say was the severest and longest battle ever fought. For 3 weeks I lived in a hole in the ground with my General and about 30 others. Sleep except for a few hours at a time was impossible-a wash was out of the question. Day and night shells rained around us – 2 bursting on the edge of our dugout, killing a man and wounding 6 within a few yards of me. Many a time I was sent up to the front line in the battle – how I escaped I shall never understand – anyhow here I am still-and for the moment in safety in rear of the line.

I was close alongside the Leicestershire Yeomanry during one day of the battle – I am afraid they must have lost very heavily.

Well, how is Mrs Kilby and Old Birstall –I look forward to the day when I shall next see my old home again. I know however that it is in the best of hands and well looked after.

How is the house getting on in the paddock –it should be about finished by now –also have they started building on the cinder road and next to Dawes yet.

When you next see Mr George you might tell him from me that he ought to write to me sometimes.

The war seems a long way from the end as yet – but I should not be surprised to find the Germans crack quite suddenly one of these days – at least I hope they will.

Were many rooks shot this year? And did Mr Fielding Johnson shoot any on his part of the rookery?

Give my love to Mrs Kilby hoping that you and Wardle and Lewis are well.

Arthur C. Clarke.

The reference to the house in the Paddock was, I believe, that of The Close in School Lane, which was being built for Mr I Bowler. The cinder road would be Roman Road and Mr Dawes was building his house called 'Hillsborough' at what is now 41 Roman Road. The Rookery that was shared between Col. Clarke and Fielding Johnson was the Spinney at the top of School Lane. The drive through the Spinney was used for all trades vehicles, the Main Drive, being reserved for private vehicles and coaches, which ran from the Lodge at the end of The Drive (between 517 &519 Loughborough Road.), to The Hall on what is now called Roman Road. The reference to 'Wardle' was to the deputy head gardener and Lewis was Arthur and Lizzie Kilby's son. (my father).

1916 A terrible blizzard in March resulted in nearly all the trees (mostly Ash) in School Lane being blown down.

Alfred Wood, the 6 Year old, son of a farmer at Birstall Lodge Farm, was killed when the horse that he was leading went out of control and he was crushed underneath the wheels of the wagon.

1918 The Women's Institute in Birstall was founded. Officers for the inaugural year were Mrs Fielding Johnson and Miss Went. Over the years their members have diligently collected items of local interest in the form of press cuttings and have kept these in a series of scrapbooks. Some of the older ones are in the safe keeping of the 'Birstall and District Local History Society'.

1919 After the 'Great War' had ended some soldiers went to Russia with an expeditionary force. One such village man, John Green, on his return was approached by Mr G. Bouskell and asked where he had been. He was heard to reply that he had been to Vladivostok. "Oh! And where is that?" asked Mr Bouskell. "I don't know, Sir," said Green, "but it's t'other side of Syston."

Canon James Went retired, after 42 years, as Headmaster of the Wyggeston School. He had been the first headmaster of what was then the Wyggeston Hospital Boy's School in 1877. His successor as Head was Tommy Kingdom. So the saying was created that "Jimmy Went - Kingdom come".

On the 30th September Thomas Fielding Johnson Snr. was awarded the Honorary Freedom of the City of Leicester. The first such award made since Leicester became a City. He was 91 years old at the time. Thomas Snr, never actually lived at Birstall, it was his son Thomas junior who lived at The Goscote Hall.

1920 – 1929

1920 The main road to Loughborough had the 'Red Hill' summit levelled off. The result was a wide deep cutting from Station Rd. to beyond Park Rd.

1921 The population of the village at this year's census was 796 (30% up since 1901).

The War Memorial was dedicated on the 5th March. Major General Sir A.R.Hoskins, carried out the unveiling ceremony.

1922 Hannah Clarke built the 6 Kensit Cottages in Park Road in memory of John Kensit, a member of the Protestant Truth Society, who had died in 1902 in Birkenhead.

Miss Sarah Ann Adler retired as Head of the Village School. She had been its head for 36 years and was extremely well respected. However, at one time, her strong political views were in conflict with those of the Rector, The Rev. R B Disney, and this did cause some problems. It was her view that the Church should direct its political leanings toward the Tory party, which was becoming the popular political party of the day and was forming a tangible alternative to the Liberals. Not withstanding this, Canon James Went made a presentation of a Purse containing £40 to Miss Adler and the scholars and teachers (Misses Shelton and Pickaver) presented Miss Adler with a handbag. Miss Adler's successor as head of the school was Mr F Bowrah who proved to be a very enterprising person. He took a school party to Wembley for the 1923 Empire Exhibition and organised a school cricket team that played home and away fixtures with other schools.

Miss Sarah Ann Adler for 36 years Head of the village school

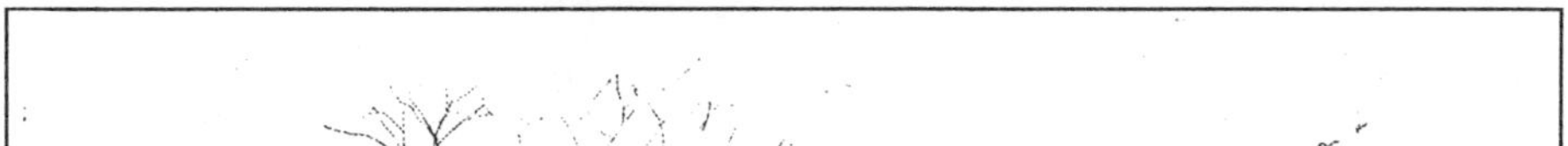

The Cottage, Front Street. Frank Garner's residence in the 1930s.

The slopes, Birstall Road. Site of the first houses built on Birstall Hall parkland.

1934 No. 39 Curzon Avenue with my mother and sister Beryl. The Council had just put up a new fence after the line of Roman Road had been agreed. This was the "Hall Gardens Cottage". The impressive Wellingtonia Fir was removed in 1960 when the house was altered.

Old Tom, Young Tom and young Tom's son Bill Sibson.

The Sibsons are Birstall's oldest surviving family. Sibson Lane was named after Tom Sibson Snr.

James Went, of The Cottage School Lane. First Head of The Wyggeston Boy's School

Birstall's Post Office in 1938. This is now the video shop at the corner of The Wayne Way

The wings of an aeroplane on a long trailer passing through the road block that is under construction on the main road at the bottom of Greengate Lane

The first 'Old English Fair' was held in the grounds of 'The Lawn'. It became an annual event, initially aiming to generate funds toward a house for Birstall's curate. £600 was raised.

1923 Following the 1922 Old English Fair Mrs Ada de Bathe, absentee owner of the Lawn estate, donated £125 toward the sum raised.

Birstall Hall, having been empty for 6 or 7 years was demolished. This work was done single handed by one man, Jim Wardle, the son of the one time Gamekeeper who was employed at The Lawn House. He was able to build a house for himself and his wife Cissie, by using the materials from the Hall. The Georgian chimney pots, on the house at 48 Curzon Avenue, which Jim called 'Crispdene' after the Crisp Clarke family, still look most impressive. Most of the other bricks etc. from the Hall, were used by George Duxbury to build several houses on Curzon Avenue at numbers 1, 9 & 22 for himself and his family. Mr Arthur Kilby, the former head gardener, was responsible for selling off the plots of land on what was left of the Hall Estate. It was necessary for him to liaise with the solicitors for the Estate, who were in London. Their senior partner was Lord Curzon of Kedleston Hall in Derbyshire. Lord Curzon was also the Secretary of State for Foreign Affairs in the government of 1923. As well as this he had also been Viceroy of India. All the avenues around the former estate were allocated names associated with persons or places that were connected with Birstall Hall and it was my grandfather's privilege to have Kilby Avenue named after him.

The Hall was not a particularly good looking building, although it was built of Georgian brick, but the surrounding Park Land was magnificently sited with extensive views over both the city of Leicester and the Soar valley. There were in the grounds some magnificent trees. The Cedar of Lebanon (circa 1710) is still very handsome. Before 1822, when the owner at that time was John Mansfield, the main turnpike road passed immediately in front of the Hall. John Mansfield had the road moved to its present position and also built an entrance Lodge at the end of the new Drive. It was at this time that the 'New Road' and bridge over the River Soar and Canal were constructed.

Mr Waterhouse Reynolds sold The Holt this year and the sale, including 'The Chantry House', (now known as "The Cottage") was held on the 30th May. Mr William Benson, of Benson's Boxes, purchased the whole of the site, which included land where 'Park House' was later to be built. He, like Mr Walker, built a superior dwelling on the land and named it 'Holly Hayes'. He used the original entrance to The Holt for the drive to his new house. The Holt was then sold to the Leicestershire County Council for a 'Children's Home' and this in itself has provided an on going story. Mr Waterhouse Reynolds, who was a Member of Parliament, was a Quaker, who at Christmas Time, would not allow traditional carols to be sung at his front door and so it was prearranged that the Carol Singers from the village should sing something different. Instead they sang a Song called "Old Black Cat".

The New Birstall Cricket Club, under their President T. G. Hirst, held their first annual dinner at the Leicester Constitutional Club. Amongst the entertainers was Master Reg Smith on the piano and Mr Jack Rosevear, toe dancer.

1924 An epidemic of 'Foot and Mouth' in the country caused cattle in Birstall, belonging to Mr Fielding Johnson, at Lodge Farm, to be destroyed. Lodge Farm was to the rear of Goscote Hall, between where Copeland Rd & Johnson Rd are now. Apparently the smell of the burning carcasses was terrible! The epidemic started in 1923, but was not officially ended until June this year.

Eclipse Buses ran their first service from the village to Leicester. George Branston founded the company, with one bus. By the late twenties, at the time the company was taken over by Kemp and Shaw, they owned six buses.

1925 The first evidence of development in Birstall, since Victorian times, was this year when Beechfield and Firfield Avenues and four houses on Sibson Rd. were built by Mr Hartshorn. Sand was extracted in large quantities for house building, from the Wanlip Lane and the Curzon Avenue parts of the village. Albert Hunt bought the turf from the lawns of Birstall Hall and sold it to the new house holders in Beechfield Avenue, who are alleged to have the 'best back lawns in Birstall'

Bert Cole built houses in The Crossways, Wanlip Avenue and some on Sibson Road. Later he built more houses in Hill Rise, The Retreat, The Wayne Way and The Meadway. The asking price for a new house was £450! Although some on Sibson Road were priced at £655. More houses were built on the lower part of Gwendolin Avenue. Mr G W Innocent opened a grocers and general hardware shop at the bottom of Gwendolin Avenue. This later became a Ladies and Gents Hairdressers run by his son, Eric. There was a Recreation Ground at the top of the avenue. A note in the Parish Council Minutes states that children under the age of 14 were not to be allowed the use of the apparatus on the 'Recky'!

On the 22nd July, Thomas Fielding Johnson Jnr. became the second member of that family to be awarded an honorary Freedom of the City of Leicester. Birstall's second Honorary Freeman of Leicester was Canon James

Went M.A. who was also bestowed with the honour at the same ceremony at the Town Hall.

1926 According to the Church Fair programme the new vicarage for St. James was finished and dedicated on 21st July by the Bishop of Peterborough. The Parish began to sever its connections with Belgrave and the Village became an Ecclesiastical Parish in its own right. The first incumbent of the new vicarage was the Rev. F. W. Walker, who although having been in the post for some considerable time was not inducted until the 26th June 1928. Geoffrey Gibson comments that Birstall had been ecclesiastically linked with Belgrave right up until 1927. The Vicar of Belgrave, the Rev. D. E. K. Llewellyn was at that time also the vicar of Birstall. However, for three years prior to this, the Rev. Frederick William Walker had been a full time 'priest in charge'. The Rev. Walker was a former Chaplain in the army, and remained in Birstall until 1935, when he exchanged livings with the vicar of Hugglescote, the Rev C G Thornton.

The houses on Kedleston Avenue and two on Curzon Avenue were erected by Frank Garner. It is interesting to note that his foreman Jack Scott was the father of Shirley Scott. Originally the cul-de-sac of twelve houses was to have been called Garner Avenue, but instead was named after Kedleston Hall where the Lord Curzon lived.

1927 The Methodists made preparations to move away from White Horse Lane. With the generous help of an interest free loan from Mr Horace Hallam, land on Wanlip Lane was purchased. But, before the sale could go ahead for £450, the Parish Council needed to find an alternative site for the Village Cricket Ground. The Fielding Johnson family made the bottom field on School Lane available and later on provided a first class pavilion.

There was more housing built on Wanlip Avenue, and also parts of Sibson Road by Bert Cole.

The inaugural meeting, of the Women's Bright Hour took place in the schoolroom underneath the Methodist Chapel. This was an interdenominational meeting for ladies of the village, with members coming from both the Anglican and Methodist Churches.

Legal papers relating to the 'Clarke Estate' included the following statement referring to the house named 'Crispdene' at 48 Curzon Avenue. *'The estate office, Crispdene shall be retained for the use by J Wardle and his wife for life and thereafter be conveyed to George Hodges Crisip Clarke or his two sons'.*

1928 The Rev. F. W. Walker was inducted as Vicar of Birstall and Rector of Wanlip (or was it the other way round?) on the 26th June. The Rev. Robert Disney who had been Vicar of Belgrave cum Birstall left and the new vicar of Belgrave was the Rev D. E. K. Llewellyn.

The Village School and Reading Room were no longer large enough for schooling purposes and so the Leicestershire Education Committee, purchased land on Wanlip Lane. A large wooden Hut, that had been a First World War Hospital building, was erected in the top corner. This comprised 4 Classrooms, Head Teachers office and a Store Room. It was used as the Junior and Senior School whilst the original school was retained until 1936 for the Infants. Before 1929 the Infant School (5-7) was in the Reading Room in Birstall Road. (formerly known as Education Road, as far as the junction with Church Hill). The Head Teacher of the Infants was Miss Athow, who was noted for being very strict. The remainder of the village children, up to the age of 14 were taught in the Church School. The Headmaster up to 1928 was Mr F Bowrah, whose daughter Miss Maisie Bowrah taught infants in Birstall up to the 60's or 70's. Other teachers were Miss Pickaver and Miss Burrell. Leonard Smith, who had previously been deputy head at Shepshed, succeeded Mr Bowrah as headmaster.

Although not in the Parish of Birstall, there were some Homestead bungalows built at the end of Greengate Lane. Apparently when Queen Victoria and Prince Albert passed through Leicester, on the 7th December 1843, on their way back from Belvoir Castle, the Queen was shocked to note the poor state of many of the people of Leicester and arranged for a sum of money to be deposited for the poor of the town. For many years this was untouched and because of the inquisitive nature of Ald. Amos Sherriff, in the early twenties, he found that this money had been deposited all those years earlier. It was agreed to use this, now considerable amount, to provide accommodation and land for some unemployed people. Ald. Amos Sherriff had been elected Mayor of Leicester in 1922, when he was 66 years old, having risen from very humble beginnings. He was a champion of the poor, never went to a school himself and started work in a brickyard at the age of six. He instigated improvements to the welfare system and it was at this time that the Ministry of Health introduced a scheme whereby unemployed men were given a number of hours work per week, according to the size of their families. It was this benevolent attitude that led him to recommend that four pairs of wooden semi-detached bungalows be built at the top of Greengate Lane, on part of the Corporation Farm land, for some of Leicester's unemployed. Along with the allocation of these dwellings came a supply of tools and equipment to enable the 'smallholders' to commence cultivating the strips of land at the rear of the dwellings. At one time these parcels of land went as far back as 'Bamber's Wood', where the new A46 dual carriageway now runs. Another councillor, Isaac Harrison, the well-known seed merchant, donated quantities of seed in order for the occupiers to grow their first crops. By 1933 four more bungalows were added but were built of brick The City Council had appealed to the Building Contractors of Leicester and most of the materials were provided, either free or very cheaply. It is only recently that the City Council tried to re-house the last few occupants. However, this pressure for re-housing met with resistance and John Charles, (still a current occupier), sought the help of John Major, the Prime Minister at the time, and letters were exchanged, with the City Council, that endorsed the original covenant and to date the remaining occupiers still enjoy their tenancies.

There were two private preparatory schools in the village. Miss Margaret Dawes B.A. opened 'Hillsborough' private school, at 41 Roman Road this year, and upon marriage to a Mr Kenney moved to 59 Curzon Avenue. This later, relocated in the Church Hall. The second private school opened in the 1920's was run by Miss Florence M. Henson, at 52 Cliffe Road. Both Schools had excellent records, preparing children for the Grammar School entrance examinations.

1929 A mammoth Summer Fair was organised by the Methodist Church on the School Lane field. This helped to provide funds to begin building their new church on Wanlip Lane and an impressive stone laying ceremony was held on the 14th September.

Victoria Cottages at the side and rear of the Reading Room were demolished. The rear walls of the houses and an occasional fireplace are still visible. The occupants were rehoused in the 14 new council houses built by Frank Garner, the local builder, for the Barrow upon Soar RDC, on Wanlip Lane at numbers 108 to 134. Frank Garner had his own sand pits on Curzon Avenue.

Houses on Holt Road, except for the top eight with first floor bays, were built this year by Harry Slater.

1930 – 1939

1930 The carved figure of a 'Saxon Beast', reputed to be about a thousand years old, was discovered in the south wall of the Parish Church.

Mr Arthur Kilby opened the New Methodist Church on Wanlip Lane and Mr Tom Sibson Snr. opened the Schoolroom on the 28th June. On completion of the new building, the Methodists sold the small parcel of land at the top of White Horse Lane to Strettons Derby Ales Brewery (SDA).

1931 The population of the village was now 3131. This was an increase of 290% since 1921.

In the upper class of the Junior School 7 successful pupils passed the scholarship to a Grammar School. For several weeks before the examinations Leonard Smith, the headmaster conducted mock exams using papers set for previous years. One of his favourite expressions – "you will get one like this (meaning a question) in the scholarship – I've just had a message from the local office and….".

In 1931 the Senior Section of the School, in the wooden hut on the Wanlip Lane, was transferred to the new Upper School at Thurmaston. Initially it was called Roundhill Central School, but later, after the Spens report, became Roundhill Modern School. Birstall pupils were bussed daily via Wanlip by Midland Red Bus. The bus had to stop each side of the 'humped canal' bridge at the 'Hope and Anchor', to remove the runners between the front and rear wheels otherwise the bus would get stuck over the top of the hump!

The Leicester Mercury reported that balloons released at the Birstall Old English fair had been recovered from Namur and Herck de Stad in Belgium.

1932 Burley Houses were built on Tempest Road from funds set up as a Trust from the estate of John Burley who had resided, many years earlier, in the 1880's, at 'The Grange' on Birstall Road. John's father was a veterinary surgeon, practising in Leicester, with his house and vets yard at the lower end of Rutland Street. It was one of several houses on the site, later to be occupied by the warehouse of Messrs Freeman Hardy Willis, which was eventually destroyed in 1940 by incendiary bombs. John, whose father was reputed to be very wealthy, died in Leamington and left £123,048 gross (£66,555net). The legacies were a complete surprise to the beneficiaries. He left £21,000, certain furniture and his two dogs, to his 'faithful' housekeeper; £5,000 to the Leicester Infirmary; £2,000 to the Leicester Institute for the Blind and £2,000 to the Children's Hospital in Leicester. The residue was left to establish homes for the widows and daughters of professional men. There are twelve self-contained houses and two bungalows together with an imposing Board Room. The houses have a wonderful view of the City and are, as John Burley had requested, exclusively for the use of widows or daughters of Leicester professional business gentlemen. Incidentally, Tempest Road gets its name from Mr Tempest Wade, a close neighbour of John Burley in the 1880's, and a very keen hunting man who had lived at Cliff House, Birstall.

A problem in the village with rats, mostly by the river caused the Parish Council to organise 'a rat hunt'. On the afternoon of Saturday 12 November. Jim 'Snap' Green, who was a popular character, along with his terrier dog, was duly appointed Village Rat Catcher. The Parish Council, represented by Councillors Ernest Dalby and

Arthur Coates, witnessed the extermination of 8 rats. The Leicester Mercury of Monday 14th November included a full cartoon feature of the episode. Later on, in May 1937, Jim and his dog 'Nip' were busy again, and this time they disposed of 131 rats, on one Sunday afternoon near to the 'Hope and Anchor' public house at Wanlip. Later on during the following week, Snap was interviewed on the BBC Radio regarding his dog's achievement. Jim was a very popular character, he had been a Sergeant in the army in the First World War having served and survived the contentious Gallipoli campaign in 1915. For many years Jim lived in the first house on Front Street, opposite to the Mill, where his Father in Law William (Billy) Wells had lived. Billy was the village Road Man and was also responsible for lighting and maintaining the Gas Lamps. Besides this he was also an accomplished carpenter, and made many a fine piece of furniture. Jim, (Snap), married Billy's daughter Emma and they had one daughter Christine Beattie, now Mrs Timmis, who still lives in Birstall in Iris Avenue. Jim was also a valuable member of the Birstall Cricket Team, being quite a notable batsman. On one occasion, where 'an all or nothing' situation came up he skied a ball right out of the ground and into the garden of 'The Close' on the opposite side of School Lane. They never did find the ball!

Also on cricket, the Leicester Evening Mail, (date unknown, pos mid 1930's), printed a letter from a Mr Johnson of Birstall, in which he describes a rather remarkable over he saw in local cricket last week. Mr. Johnson writes, "I had the pleasure of witnessing one of the most remarkable overs I have ever seen in local cricket during the Birstall v. Bowman's XI match last week on the School Lane ground, Birstall".
"E. Sibson, an old stalwart of the Birstall Club, and a left arm bowler, captured four wickets in five balls due mainly

to the vigilance of J. McKenna, the ex Leicester City goalkeeper, who was keeping wicket for Birstall. The first two balls of the over were taken smartly to stump two men. The third delivery split a double hat trick for Sibson and McKenna, while the fourth and fifth balls provided another couple of victims for McKenna. Again fate robbed these two players of a hat trick, for the sixth ball was edged for a run, but the ball was returned smartly to the wicket keeper who whipped off the bails before the batsman got home. Hard luck for the Sibson and McKenna combination, but congratulations on a splendid piece of work".

Many who remember Ernest Sibson will have acknowledged his prowess as a left arm bowler. Had it not been for a severe war wound, in which his left arm was badly damaged, he could have been playing for the County, as I believe he had had a trial with them before the 1914-18 War.

1933 The Municipal boundary was moved and houses between the Red Hill roundabout and parts of Tempest Road, Roman Road, Curzon Avenue and Birstall Road were administratively transferred from the County to the City of Leicester. This area was, thanks to the efforts of Leslie Dolman, Clerk to the Barrow-upon-Soar RDC, returned to the County in 1963.

Goscote Hall, which had been built in 1841, and originally called 'Birstall Hill House' was sold this year after the death of Mrs Fielding Johnson.

1934 The Goscote estate was developed by Harry Slater, who was later financed by Mr William Benson of 'Benson Box Co. and of 'Holly Hayes' The roads on the estate were named after local personalities – Walker Rd after the then

Vicar, Went Rd after Canon Went, Fielding and Johnson Roads after the former owners. Copeland Rd was named after John Coupland (why they never spelt it correctly, nobody knows!) The houses fronting Loughborough Rd (opposite the playing fields/cricket ground) were built by, amongst others, Burrows of Leicester who also developed parts of the Goscote Hall estate. Quite a number of the houses on the Goscote estate were built by J C W Stacey. He was responsible for the tile fronted houses on Fielding Road, some of Johnson Road and two pairs of semis on Park Road extension as well as the house called 'Brackley', No. 61, which he built for himself. Many of the houses on Oakfield, Elmfield and the smaller roads off, were designed by Charlie Haines and built by 'Bill' Jarvis. The even numbered houses on Windmill Avenue, the houses on Acacia Avenue and the lower end of Stonehill Avenue, were built by William Davis.

The large house called 'The Lawn' was sold for development to a company consisting of Tempest-Bouskell (solicitor) John C W Stacey (builder), Quail (builder) and Fred Smith (Inland Revenue Officer!!).

1935 The Rev C G Thornton succeeded the Rev F W Walker as vicar of Birstall. The verger at the Parish Church in the 1920's & 30's was Mr John Parkes, who lived in 'The Rookery' in Netherhall Lane. He was a small kindly man with rosy cheeks who took his duties very seriously. John had served in the Boer War and was at the relief of Mafeking on 17th May 1900. The Churchwardens were – Vicars Warden, Mr George E Bouskell, people's warden Mr S W Wilkinson. Mr Bouskell was a solicitor and also the Coroner. Mr Wilkinson had small engineering business in Western Rd. Leicester. Later, Mr. Wilkinson was succeeded as warden, by Mr. W F B Smith of Church Hill. The choirmaster and organist from 1928 was Mr Wilf.

Burnett who was on the staff of Taylor's Bell Foundry at Loughborough, having moved to Birstall from Gainsborough. Prior to the arrival of Mr Burnett, the choirmaster was the vicar. Still remembered are the special choir practices for Easter, which took place at the Vicarage on Sunday morning at 10 o'clock before the morning service at 11am. The Church seated just 216 and as the village grew so did the congregations and by the mid thirties there would be as many as six services on Easter Sunday. Holy Communion at 6.15 am, 7 & 8, Sung Eucharist at 11, Children's Service at 2.45 pm and Evensong at 6.30 pm. For the evening service it was necessary to arrive at the church by at least 6.10 pm or else you would not get a good seat! Later, there was another service added at 9.30 am!

Neville Turner of Stonehill Avenue, age five, fell 40 feet from the bridge on Station Road on to the platform of Birstall Station on 23rd August. He was taken to Loughborough on a train that was drawing into the station as he fell. On reaching Loughborough Hospital he was reported to be in a critical condition. I regret that I do not know his fate!

1936 The company that bought the Lawn House and its ancillary buildings, developed the site and the other side of Wanlip Lane, near the Triangle. Stacey's built The Lawn Cinema for George Cockcroft, who owned several other cinemas in the county. He also built the Social Club, whilst Slater built Lawn Avenue and some houses on the Wanlip Lane. A garage was established at the north side of the Cinema and was operated originally by Frank Brayshaw, a pioneer motor engineer who later with Alvis Cars and Citroen Cars operated from Loughborough Rd Belgrave, where Lidl is now situated. Fred Smith, the Inland Revenue Officer eventually left Birstall for London where he became

Comptroller General of the Inland Revenue. (I'm told that on occasional visits back to Birstall he was still to be seen in his old overcoat!).

The 'Lawn' building of the Birstall Riverside School was opened this year, for the junior children, whilst the infants from the Church Hall were transferred to the wooden hut. Mr Leonard Smith was still the headmaster. He himself taught the scholarship class (later to be known as the 11 plus). A strong believer in the three R's he worked hard to get as many scholarship passes as possible. There was no Secondary School in Birstall until 1955 and children who passed the 11 plus exam went to, Loughborough Grammar, Loughborough College , Loughborough High School for girls, or Rawlin's Grammar School at Quorn. However if you resided in that part of Birstall that was in the City, you had a choice between The Wyggeston Boys, The Gateway, The City Boys or Alderman Newton's Boys or Alderman Newton's Girls. There was also The Collegiate Girls' but this was mostly a fee paying school. However, some grammar school entrants living in the 'county part' of the village did go to schools in the City.

The Church Hall, no longer to be used as a school, was converted to an all purpose 'Village Hall' with splendid facilities for drama presentations and was dedicated by the Bishop on the 13th June. During the months of conversion, the builder George Rudkin, installed a super sprung dance floor.

Canon James Went died aged 91. He was a lay Canon at Leicester Cathedral and Freeman of Leicester. Albert Hunt purchased his three-wheeler tricycle, at the sale of contents of the house! The Cottage, which is the oldest dwelling in the Village, having been built in the 15th century, may have been the Friars House to Leicester Abbey, and was also reputed to once have been three properties, being possibly at one time, a Georgian Farm and two houses. It was rumoured to have had an underground tunnel that led to St. James Church. On the death of Canon Went the house was sold to Mark Taylor but in 1946 was sold again, and this time the purchasers were Mr and Mrs William G. Fox. Bill Fox became a Colonel during the 2nd World War and his wife Peggy was the daughter of Mr T G Hirst of 'The Old Elms' Birstall Road.

Fairs were held annually during the first week of August, in the fields by the river at the bottom of Whiles Lane. The Fair was set to coincide with the Patronal Festival of St James on the 25th July, but since 1752, when this country adopted the Gregorian calendar, Fairs all over the land were, and still are, about 11 days late. September 3rd was followed by September 14th. Britain also adopted January 1st as the day when a new year begins. This eleven days shortage caused many problems, not the least being that when Lady Day (25th March) came around in 1753, peasants refused to pay their annual rents etc. Because of this inequitable situation people were from then on, allowed to pay them 11 days later on the 5th April, which is the date the Tax Year still ends! America also changed its calendar at the same date. George Washington, was born on 11th February 1732, but from 1753 onwards always celebrated his birthday on the 22nd February, which is still remembered in America as 'Presidents Day'.

12th September was the date the Social Club was opened on a site adjacent to the recently demolished 'Lawn Hall'.

The Lawn Cinema opened on the 5th October, but the official opening was two weeks later on the 19th. There was a Laurel and Hardy film 'The Bohemian Girl' and a performance by the Leicester Accordian Band. Public

Nuisance No. 1' with Francis Day, 'Remember Last Night' with Laurel and Hardy and 'Alibi Inn' with Molly Law were other early films on at the 'Lawn'. The new manager was Bert Pollard.

Jimmy Wardle, the former deputy head gardener and agent of the Clarke Estate died on the 31st October. His father, John Wardle had been the last working gamekeeper in Birstall.

In the autum the St. James Guild of Youth Choir was formed with Wilf Burnett as the conductor. They gave their first concert in the Parish Church on the 21st November. It was exceptionally well received.

King George V died, and Edward VIII abdicated. On the 12th December the Duke of York became George VI. Children who went carol singing at Christmas were accused of irreverently changing the words to the second line of 'Hark, the herald angels sing' by substituting it with, 'Mrs Simpson's pinched our King'

1937 The Birstall British Legion was formed at No.19 Front Street and proved to be a very successful branch. Since their inception they have won the Earl Haig Cup, which is awarded annually to the national branch showing the most exceptional progress and efficiency, no less than 5 times in 1938, 39, 50, 55 & 57.

King George VI and Queen Elizabeth were crowned in Westminster Abbey on the 12th May.

Miss Adler died on July 1st. 15 years after she had retired as headmistress of the village school.

A 'Barnstormer' came to the Co-op playing fields on Birstall Road and gave five-shilling flights in an old Avro biplane.

Harry Slater built six new shops on the village end of Sibson Road and the first occupiers were: Mr Atkins (Fish Shop), Mr Kenney (Ironmongers), Mr Cartwright (Lawn Stores, Sweets & General), Geoff. Lane (Butcher), Mrs Mabel Joyce (Groceries), and Mrs Bouchard (Haberdashery). Mr Atkins had moved from his original shop, across the Road, in what is now the Taxi Company. Mrs Swann converted the front room of the original Lodge to 'The Lawn' (now a Kebab Shop) into a Sweet Shop.

1938 The Village Post Office and General Grocery shop at 53 Front Street was sold to the Catholic Church to be used as a Presbytery. At one time Mr Cufflin, a former shopkeeper, had a load of ice blocks fall from the lorry and they rolled down Whiles Lane, into the river and began floating toward Thurmaston. Another time a whole box of fireworks caught fire in the shop and this too had disastrous results! When the shop was sold, the Post Office had to be relocated and this was taken over by George Cook at 121 Sibson Road (currently the Video shop). The other occupiers of the adjoining shops at this end of Sibson Rd. were, Philip Stone (Chemist), Worthington's (Grocers), Sketchley's (Cleaners), Andrews' Fish Shop, (the altered chimney arrangement for the Fish & Chip fryer, can still be seen above Birstall Jewellers). The next shop was Bowman's the Butchers and the 'Off Licence' was owned by Hartopps. Then came Taylor's Sweet Shop, currently where Mr Shar has his Dental Practice. Karl K Toone, the greengrocer was next, then Harold and Ethel Moody's Ladies and Gents Hairdressers. Greasley's bread shop and Furburrows wool shop completed the line of shops from The Wayne Way to the end of the service road. At this time there were only two shops between The Crossways and Wanlip Avenue and they were Pearns, the newsagents and Laundons, a ladies and gents outfitters. They are where Supacare and Tomorrows World Travel are at the present time. Across on the Wanlip Avenue corner was Wintertons the grocers where Fresh Approach is now. There were two semi-detached houses and two bungalows and two more semis where Patricks, The Take Away, The Pet Shop, the RSPCA, Coombs and the Charity Shop are. Where Hobbits was in 1999, was previously a Milk Bar, run by Stafford Bentley, but long before that it was a Bicycle shop run by Mr Newham. In The Crossways there was the Number 40 branch of the Leicestershire Co operative Society, with its separate Butchery department next door. I well remember going with my mother and leaving an order for our groceries that was delivered next day in a brown paper parcel. When paying for our goods we always quoted our Co op number '1646' then in January the following year we would go to Union Street in Leicester and collect our dividend. I also remember we purchased our Milk and Bread checks from the Crossways shop.

October saw the completion of the proposals for a Village Cemetery at the top of Greengate Lane.

An Olde English Fair on the School Lane Fields involved the whole of the Village. This was organised to raise funds for the Parish Church extensions but, because of the War years, plans were postponed and then later, completely altered. The enlargement was eventually finished in 1962.

The new automatic telephone exchange at the bottom of Johnson Road was opened in the Autumn. All the Birstall numbers were given a prefix (84) e.g. No. 46 became 84046. The new exchange was fully automatic and was able

1938

to cope with the 350 to 400 lines that had previously been managed by several full time operators at Front Street.

The Infant School on Wanlip Lane (Orchard Building) was built and opened in time for the winter term 1939. Miss Athow was still the Headmistress with Miss Fazey, as senior mistress. The Wooden Hut still remained and was in use for many years afterwards. Because of the continued increase in the population class sizes were as high as '55'.

During the 1930's Sir Alan Cobham's circus came to the fields on part of the Golf Club. You could pay 5 shillings and have a 'flip' in an aeroplane from the field off Park Road, behind about No. 84 where Jim Cartwright lived. Many a World War II pilot had his flying appetite whetted by a visit to one of these exhibitions.

On the 28th January there was a practice black out in the village and later on a Territorial army recruiting demonstration, with searchlights, was held on the School Lane field.

Bert Smith, the village blacksmith bought Miss Adler's house, next to the Reading Room.

There was a mock Air raid and black out practice on the 13th July.

Snow White and the Seven Dwarfs was one of the feature films at the Lawn Cinema.

Horace Hallam's haystack burned to the ground. He lost fifty tons of hay.

Wanlip Hall, which was against the Church, and the Rectory at the corner of Rectory Road and Wanlip Lane

German Prisoners of War picking potatoes on Ralph Hallam's field in 1944. Sam Boulter, Ralph's farm manager, is driving the tractor. The house in the distance is 751, Loughborough Road.

1944, Ralph Hallam with Ted Woolaston and George Walton "brussel knobbing". Roy Greasley is in the background.

1945 VE Day party for Paget Avenue area.

*Lawn Cinema, Kenney's Ironmongers and the Fish Shop.
The Motor Repair Garage, originally used by Frank Brayshaw,
is next door to the cinema.*

"Birstall Legionnaires" circa 1946

8th June 1946. Birstall British Legion garden party at The Elms on Birstall Road. Platform party: Mrs. Dalby, Rev. Dick Connell and Phyllis, Rev. Francis Pratt, Mrs. Mawby, Bert Moore, Lord Mayor Ald. William Henry Smith and Mrs. Smith, Mrs. Baldock, Miss F. M. Henson and Mrs. Cotton.

See P63

Kemp and Shaw buses Nos.22 and 23 at St. Margaret's Bus Station. The special low double decker was designed for the Derby route.

Via Barkby Bridge — See P63

were both demolished. Wanlip has a long and memorable history and I have included items that I hope you will find interesting in **Appendix I** at the end of this diary.

1939 – 1945 The War Years

1939 Many of us remember exactly where we were when we were told that war had been declared against Germany. We at the Methodist Church had a new Minister start that day. The Rev. John Henry Fenton included the baptism of baby Christine Hallam, daughter of Kathleen and Ralph Hallam in the morning service on the 3rd September and because of the news of the impending declaration, relatives who had travelled long distances were encouraged to return home as quickly as possible. These supporters or God Parents, as they were called, went home to Hertfordshire and were replaced by other friends and relatives who resided more locally and acted as proxies. News that war had been declared was passed on to the minister, just after 11 o'clock, by Frank Bryant, the church steward, who had waited at home for the all important news broadcast, by Mr Neville Chamberlain, the Prime Minister.

The country was in turmoil! Thinking that we were all going to be bombed the very next day. Air Raid Shelters were constructed as quickly as possible. There were three main types: One was erected inside a hole dug in the back garden. It had a corrugated iron roof that was covered with soil and was called an Anderson shelter after John Anderson who became Chancellor of the Exchequer in 1943. A Morrison shelter was like an inverted iron bedstead and was usually located in the front room of your house. The Morrison shelter was named after Herbert Morrison who was Home Secretary in 1940 and Deputy Prime Minister in 1945. The third type was the street shelter built of brick with heavily reinforced concrete roofs. People who did not have a satisfactory shelter at home were allocated space in one.

1940 – 1949

1940 To reiterate the widespread uncertainty and confusion that existed, I well recall the times the siren, on top of the Goscote Hall, sounded and we had to get to an Air Raid Shelter as quickly as possible. I know of one Birstall family that hurried to the shelter on Wanlip Lane, between the Social Club and Lawn Avenue the first time they heard the siren, but on the way realised that they had left the budgerigar in the cage at home. The son in law was quickly dispatched back home and he was able to deal with the unfortunate bird, by wringing its neck and so avoid it being killed by a German bomb! Imagine their distress on returning home after the 'all clear' had sounded and finding the bird dead at the bottom of the cage! Apparently this sort of thing happened all over the country. Even London Zoo had a team of six keepers, with rifles, who were ready to shoot any large carnivorous animal that, in the event of the zoo being bombed, could possibly escape. Many Vets' practices were inundated by the large number of dead animals that were left on their doorsteps.

The air raid shelters at the Junior and Primary schools, which were all underground, were not completed by the first day of term in 1940 and because of this the whole school had an extra days Christmas holiday.

The 26th May 1940 was declared a national day of prayer and Churches remained open all day.

Air raid sirens were first sounded in Birstall at midnight on the 25th June 1940 and repeated on the next four nights. From 14th August to 31st December there were 38 Air Raid Warnings.

A 'Soldiers' tea was held at the Plough Inn, and at the height of the Battle of Britain the 'Earl of Stamford' displayed a blackboard outside on which was chalked the daily tally of enemy aircraft shot down. Vehicles all had to have their headlights replaced or covered up. A large tarpaulin sheet was placed over each railway engine to make sure the light from the fire, could not be seen by a pilot of an enemy plane. Names of towns and villages were removed and signposts taken down.

Fund Raising for the war effort began in earnest. Committees were formed for Infirmary bed appeals.

A popular Concert Party was formed from members of the British Legion, who had served in the 1914-18 War. They were called 'The Legionaires' and their first concert was held in March 1940 in the Social Club. They became quite famous and later concerts were given in 'The Lawn Cinema'. The members of the group were Steve Farmer, Norman Freestone, Ray Loakes, Bill Payne, Jim Sarson and Fred Sleath.

The Home Guard was formed mainly from men who had served in the 1914-18 war. They were originally called the Local Defence Volunteers (LDV). Their local headquarters were at 'The Grange' on Birstall Road, and many stories have been related over the years of unusual and hilarious activities undertaken. Birstall had its own Observer Corps and their post was just off the Wanlip Lane, opposite to Windmill Avenue in a specially constructed building next to the potato shed that was owned by 'Bill Luck'.

Concerts continued to be arranged in the Lawn Cinema to raise funds for either beds at the Leicester Royal Infirmary or for Battleships and even Spitfires. The Government commandeered iron railings, from the fronts of houses, and appeals were made for all kinds of old metal. Even old saucepans were needed to go to be melted down for war purposes. Rotas of Street Wardens were arranged and there was always somebody on duty at night, touring their own street or streets. First task next morning was to take the steel helmet and stirrup pump to the next person on the rota. Birstall had its own Fire Station and this was manned by the (AFS) Auxiliary Fire Service in 'Agar's Stables' (now Nelsons Packaging.) I can still remember the telephone number. It was 2222.

Everyone was issued with a gas mask and each locality had a visit by a gas inspector, in a van. This was so that we could all go into the gas filled sealed van and experience a realistic gas attack.

Roadblocks were created. I remember one was at the bottom of Greengate Lane, on the Loughborough Road and the other was at the top of Wanlip Lane, against No. 134, which at that time was the last house on the lane. This roadblock had to be redesigned to allow the three buses full of children, to go on their way to Roundhill School at Thurmaston, each day. Who would have thought that the 'Powers that be' would replace this road-block in exactly the same place in the late 1990's!

During the war the village had about 200 evacuees who were from the Brighton and Hove area. The education authority rented the Methodist Church schoolroom to accommodate these pupils. They were split into four classes of 50, with only wooden partitions separating them from each other. Some evacuees were taught in the Wooden School.

Everyone was encouraged to grow plenty of vegetables. Wide roadside verges were also used to grow potatoes and even cereal crops. The Birstall Golf Club had to plough up 9 of the 18 holes for the duration of the war. Even Victoria Park and Braunstone Park were used in the same way.

Land Army Girls played an important part in the war effort. Many Farmers were, at first, very dubious as to the practicalities of employing them for farm work but they exceeded all their expectations. There were at least 6 girls allocated to local Farmers in Birstall. Horace and Ralph Hallam employed 3 they were Francis Yates, Gladys Cousins and Joyce Lucas who was admired by Fred Forder, a builder, who had come to the Farm at Wanlip to build a new dairy, where Joyce was working. The feeling was mutual and so they eventually became married. Joyce still lives in Birstall, as does Edna Chester (nee Exton) who worked for Karl Toone. The other two were firstly, Dot Riley (nee Colbourn), another Birstall girl still in the village, who worked in the dairy at Harry Hunt's Farm in Netherhall Lane. Harry Hunt also employed some German Prisoners of War and one stayed in this country and married a girl from Thurmaston. He was named Edward Pasch and I believe he still lives in Thurmaston. Finally, there was Sylvia (Sam) Bird who worked for Frank Bass. Sam's parents lived on Wanlip Lane, next door to the School at No. 49 and were stewards for many years at the Social Club.

Price controls were introduced in all our shops and market stalls. Imported fruits were hardly ever available and Ration books were used for all sorts of supposedly fair allocation. I well remember that at the back of each little brown booklet, there were four panels. A.B.C, and D, and each time a customer was sold certain foodstuffs the panels were marked with an indelible pencil. Nearly everything was rationed. Sugar – 12ozs per week; butter/margarine – 4ozs; 8ozs of bacon; 8ozs dried fruit were allowed at Christmas. The window in Geoff Lane's shop (now David Michael's) displayed an alphabetical list, on a blackboard that was changed weekly and when your 'surname initial' came up! you were eligible for some 'offal' such as liver, kidneys or even sheep's brains! which were 'off the ration'. Eggs were also in short supply and because of this many households kept a few chickens at the bottom of their gardens. The chickens didn't smell much but the constant cooking of meal and potato peelings to feed them on was quite nauseating! Families who kept chickens were able to overcome the egg shortage, and any surplus eggs were preserved in a bucket or earthenware pancheon of isinglass and used through the winter months. One item of food that was frequently available was Spam! I well remember one particular birthday party that several of us lads went to in the early 1940's. Michael Mayes was about 11 or 12 and Mrs Mayes (Rachel) provided plate after plate of Spam sandwiches for about 10 or a dozen boys at his party in Roman Road. We scoffed the lot! We even had a competition to see who could eat the most! Where Mrs Mayes got all the Spam from I'll never know.

Very little enemy activity was experienced in Birstall. A string of unexploded incendiary bombs landed in the fields, by the river, at the bottom of Kilby Avenue, which I understand have never been found! One Land Mine fell on a house at No.3 Tollemache Avenue, just off Abbey Lane, but only a few yards from the railway. Apparently, the house that was hit belonged to the family of John Hoskins, (Midland Windows).

The nearest and possibly much less devastating was the Land Mine that dropped, again near the railway line, at the top of Greengate Lane on the 14th November 1940. The siren had gone at 9.25 pm and later that night the land mine fell in an area, which is now covered by housing, at the northern end of Fieldgate Crescent. The Crater was 20 feet deep and it was quite exciting to go searching for pieces of shrapnel. Many houses in the Village were damaged by the blast! The Stonehill Avenue area suffered quite badly in that a considerable number of the houses lost their windows. Some of the Shops on Sibson Road had their windows blown out and the Co-Op on The Crossways also had its windows shattered. One house, in Poplar Avenue, No. 26, had its front window cracked but not broken. However, the curtains were jammed in the frame of the window and the glass had to be broken in order to release the curtains. Mrs Tipping, the owner, lost buttons off her coat yet did not remember them coming off. The Land Mine was also blamed for disrupting underground springs. One air raid shelter became so badly flooded that it was no longer usable. There were two fatalities! Horace Hallam lost two sheep that were grazing in the field near to the land mine. The plane that dropped the mine was a Dornier Do 17, which crashed near to Burton on the Wolds killing all the crew of four. A second mine dropped on the other side of the railway at the same time.

Mr Philip Stone, the chemist on Sibson Road (where Boots is now) was on special constable's duty walking over the railway bridge at the time the land Mines were dropped. He was not injured but his uniform was shredded. The all-clear sounded at 5.5 am. It transpired that Coventry had suffered very badly that night and the flames from there could be seen as distant flashes and a glow in the night sky.

In contrast Kirby Muxloe was less fortunate in that only five days later, on the 19th November they suffered as many as 5 bombs on their village and for a time as many as 400 were made homeless. 200 folk were able to return soon after but 87 houses were badly damaged and of these seven were completely destroyed and were not rebuilt until 1947. These bombs were also said to have been part of a residue load destined for Coventry, or possibly destined for the nearby munitions factory at Desford.

Between 1939 and 1945 Wanlip Church rooms, formerly the Hall Stables, were used as store for war weapons that had been manufactured by Cascelloid Ltd.

Birstall had many heroes and Sgt. John Hannah who won the Victoria Cross, was probably the most famous. John was a wireless operator on a Hampden named "Bet". Flt. Lt. Joe Collier usually skippered this plane, but on this occasion, Joe was not on board the Hampden Bomber, named after his wife. In the event the raid that took place on the night of the 15-16 September 1940, included 15 Hampden Bombers of 83 Squadron who had attacked a concentration of barges near Antwerp, and "Bet" badly damaged by flak, and on fire, only just managed to get home thanks to the valiant efforts of the 18 year old John Hannah who besides being the wireless operator was also the gunner. After exhausting every fire extinguisher, John Hannah was forced to remove his facemask and suffocating in the heat, eventually beat out the flames with his logbook and hands. Because of this the aircraft returned safely and no doubt, repaired and used for further trips. At the start of the fire the pilot ordered the crew to 'bale out' and two of the crew did and were captured. John Hannah later visited the Junior School and we all went into the assembly hall to see him, and the Victoria Cross, which he was so proud to show us. At that time, he was the youngest person to receive the VC. Unfortunately, John never recovered from his injuries and he developed tuberculosis, resulting in his being discharged from the RAF in December 1942.

1941 Milk rationing started on the 14th April and in June, on the 18th & 19th the Plough Inn was closed because there was 'no beer'.

There was a war savings committee and we children at the local schools took monies for Mrs Churchill's Russian Sailors appeal fund.

Despite all the restrictions the war caused, members of the Roman Catholic faith in the village were able to build their new church on Wanlip Lane. It was completed in 1940 and the first mass was celebrated in January 1941. The church, named after St. Theresa of Lisieux was next to St. Timlocks! Many people remember Father Horgan, the first Parish Priest, with great love and affection. He remained in the village for many years. It is interesting to note that the Rosminians of Ratcliffe were the first religious order in England to abandon clerical bands in favour of what boys at school called 'back to fronts'. We now refer to these clerical collars that Priests wear, as 'dog-collars'.

The Women's section of The British Legion was also formed this year. Their first meetings were held in the Reading Room, but later on they found the Earl of Stamford was a more suitable place to meet!

1942 The A.T.C. was formed this year and still meets weekly at the Riverside School. The A.T.C. unit was B. Flight, 1462 Squadron. A number of its members were killed on wartime flying and ground duties with the R.A.F. The CO was W. B. Giles who had been a First World War fighter pilot. After fighting on the Somme in the Somerset Light Infantry he retrained in the R.F.C. and shot down five enemy aircraft. One of the Officers was Norman Wakefield from the Thurmaston group who often trained on the Riverside School playground.

1943 The gallantry of John Hannah V. C. was recognised by the people of Birstall when, on the 11th February, they organised a testimonial dance in his honour at the Birstall Social Club.

1944 The Birstall Home Guard (A Company of 1st North Leicester Battalion) stood down prior to disbanding, with a grand supper and concert at the Birstall Social club.

1945 Immediately after the war in Europe the 8th May was deemed to be V E Day and we had some super street parties. Many participants contributed one shilling per head and each street was able to provide dancing, fireworks and a sumptuous tea which was laid out on tables down the middle of the street. Everybody had a great time. Later in the year, on the 14th August, the War in the Far East ended when the Japanese agreed the terms of Surrender and the 15th was declared to be V J Day. So we all had another party.

After the war dozens of Pre-Fabricated bungalows were erected on Wanlip Lane. Later, they were replaced with more modern and permanent housing stock.

On Sunday the 18th March a terrible wind caused a great deal of damage. My father and I witnessed the collapse of the old Birstall Hall Garden vineries, which were at the back of our cottage and had been used as a large greenhouse by my grandfather and father. It was over 100ft long, 20 ft wide and 20ft high and it fell on to Curzon Avenue and caused quite a hazard. It was a massive construction with fancy wrought iron frames, typical of the latter part of the 18th century, when it was built. It took many days to clear the roadway.

The Birstall Choral Society was formed during 1945 with Louis Higginson as conductor. Other conductors after this were, Walter Pole, Sydney Newton, Richard Butt, and since 1961, Shirley Scott, until its doors closed in 2001.

1946 During the summer the village celebrated the Victory of the Second World War, over a period of four days from June 8th to the 11th. There were dozens of events at various venues throughout the village, ending at 10 p.m. on Tuesday night with a bonfire and firework display at the top of Johnson Road. On Sunday 9th June, there was a united service of thanksgiving in the main hall of the Birstall Council School, which in effect was the forerunner of all future united services in the village. Canon Francis Pratt, the Vicar of St. James and The Rev. R. J. Connell of the Methodist Church, conducted the joint 'Service of Thanksgiving for the Return of Peace'. The service concluded with the Hallelujah Chorus sung by the Birstall Choral Society.

A Birstall girl, June Slater, daughter of Harry Slater the local builder, won a beauty competition and was elected 'Princess of Industry' for the City of Leicester. June, who worked at the Wolsey on Abbey Park Road, was later in the year, introduced to King George VI and Queen Elizabeth, on the occasion of their visit to Leicester.

1947 Both the Parish Church and the Methodist Church continued to raise monies for their respective building projects. They both had popular support. As far as the Methodists were concerned, the members of the Sunday School performed annual concerts as did the Ladies Bright Hour group. The 'Men's Pantomime' was formed and a production of Cinderella was the first of many all male cast pantomimes performed from 1948 onwards. The Church's concern for Outreach was maintained throughout and at Christmas 1947 a group of youngsters went carol singing and the money raised was sent to the National Children's Home. This proved to be the beginning of a very long, and still ongoing, relationship with the N C H. Since then many thousands of pounds have been raised, and sent to this charity.

This was sadly the year that Flt/Sgt. John Hannah died. The injuries he received on that memorable night in 1940 unfortunately took their toll. He died quite young, at the age of 25, in Markfield Sanatorium on the 7th June. His widow and three daughters lived at 87 Stonehill Avenue, where Janet still lives.

Sir William Brockington CBE retired as the first Director of Education for Leicestershire. It was in 1903 that he was appointed to this post and his reputation as an astute leader of men spread far and wide. Sir William, who resided in Birstall, at 507 Loughborough Road, was renowned for many innovative schemes and ideas, including the setting up of 'The Modern School' at Roundhill. He was responsible for instigating the original 'Eleven Plus' in 1919 and was awarded the CBE in 1927 for creating 'The Little Bible', which he edited for school use, and also a 'Leicestershire Hymns and Prayers For Use In Schools', both being used nationally for many generations. He was also one of the working party that compiled the draft scheme for the 1944 Education Act, and had earlier become a pioneer for the separate education of all secondary school children.

The Princess Elizabeth was married to Prince Philip on the 20th November.

1948 The National Health Service was introduced on the 5th July.

The birth of Prince Charles was announced on the 14th November.

1949 Leicester City Football Club won through to the F. A. Cup Final at Wembley in May this year. Although they lost 3-1 to Wolves there was tremendous support for our local team especially as the Chairman of the club, Len Shipman, lived in the village. One local business that benefited by the trip to Wembley was S (Sid) F Parker, the Television and Radio Engineer from Went Road. Prior to the Saturday of the match he sold hundreds of television sets to the residents of Birstall. One Birstall man who had a television set before the 2nd world war was Mr J W Pallett of 601 Loughborough Road. He was a close friend of Mr May of Church Gate and together with a Mr Howard, who was the grandson of Mr John T Clarke (Birstall Lighthouse, Park Road) they were members of the 'Leicester Radio Society'.

One important contributor to the life of Birstall who died on the 5th May this year was Mr Thomas Shaw of 679 Loughborough Road. Many years earlier he and Mr Kemp jointly founded the well known Bus Company, Kemp and Shaw Ltd. Before moving to their Thurcaston Road premises, they ran their buses from 209 Loughborough Road, between Bath Street and The Belgrave Hotel, where Thomas and his wife, Mary Ann, had lived along side the Bus Garage. In the late 1930's a ticket from Front Street, at the top of Whiles Lane, to Garden Street, Leicester cost 3d (old pence). Children were charged half price. Allen's and Boyer's were two other private companies that ran between Leicester and Loughborough. Kemp and Shaw were successful in holding a licence to run a daily service to Derby It was in March 1947, that a disaster befell when the bridge over the River Trent, at Shardlow, was washed away by floods after heavy winter snowfalls. For some time the service was rerouted via Sawley Cross Roads before rejoining the A6 further north. A replacement Bailey Bridge installed by the Army had so little head room that the firm purchased a new double-decker, tailored to pass under the bridge's low box shaped superstructure.

Thomas's son, Thomas Arthur, was a popular bus driver. Perhaps you can remember him! He was the driver who had a distinctive 'birth mark' on the left side of his face. And do you remember the conductor, Mr Nutting, who was slightly disabled? He experienced no trouble whatsoever in climbing the stairs of a double-decker. The grandson of Thomas, Tom Arthur William Shaw, and his wife, Margaret, currently live in South Wigston. If you remember also, Allen's had a licence to run a weekly service to Skegness. These licences were very precious and at the time were much sought after by the Midland Red bus company. Two further notes regarding the Shaw family, Mrs Mary Ann Shaw was a one time president of the Belgrave Ladies Bowling Club, that met on the St. Margaret's Pastures, and Mr Shaw, having previously lived in Wigston was a member of the Wigston Brass Band, where he played a large Tuba. Mrs Shaw died in 1950 and they are both buried in the Greengate Lane cemetery. About the end of 1949 Kemp and Shaw was under an agreement of many years standing, taken over by Allens of Mountsorrel.

1950 - 1959

1950 The Council completed negotiations for the purchase of 13 acres of land off School Lane for the Village Playing Fields from the estate of the late Mr Fielding Johnson. A Playing Fields committee was formed and once more the whole village found itself involved in raising money. The contractors developing the playing fields had a very difficult task. There were so many 'springs' in the top south-west corner of the three fields that a special culvert had to be created through to the river via the Triangle and between the Lawn Cinema and the Earl of Stamford.

1951 There was no census in 1941 but the population of the village at this year's census was 6667, which shows that it had doubled since 1931.

The Playing Fields were officially opened in July by Lt. Col. Sir Robert Martin. The Bishop of Leicester dedicated the grounds and the ornate gates that were given by Mr and Mrs William Sutton of 4 Oakfield Avenue, in memory of their son Roy who had died in a motor-cycle accident in January the previous year.

The Festival of Britain took place, mostly in London, with a new Festival Hall and an impressive 'Skylon' on the south bank.

1952 On the 6th February this year King George VI died, and Elizabeth II succeacceded to the throne at the age of 25.

Annie Sutton, the last surviving dependant of Joseph Sutton, died on the 10th April. It was Joseph Sutton who rescued the old 'Red Hill Gallows' from the barn of the farm at the top of Church Hill, where `he had lived with his father William Sutton. He arranged for the old oak posts to be made into three wooden stools for his children. Apparently William had at one time rented the grazing rights of the Parkland belonging to Birstall Hall and had stored the gallows in the barn at the farm for safety. The actual site of the Gallows is not known but it is believed that they were above Hermitage Road and between the Old Turnpike road, now Roman Road, and the present Loughborough Road. Annie along with her brother Frank and younger sister Janet lived in the fairly large wooden bungalow at the top of Meadow Lane. They ran a small holding that covered the area where, in the ensuing years, the Barrow upon Soar RDC built houses on Lambourne Road, Bramley Road and Blenheim Road, and where some elderly folk's bungalows are now. Harry Slater privately developed the lower end of Bramley, Orchard and Lambourne Roads and also built the four shops on Wanlip Lane. Almost fifty years on the old five barred gate to the smallholding is still in place. It can be seen in the right hand side of the hedgerow, in Meadow Lane, behind the houses in Lambourne Road.

1953 There had been a very successful Birstall Drama Society in the village for many years, which used the Church Hall. Another group, calling themselves 'The Q.T's' was founded this year, at the Methodist Church. After an initial committee meeting at 26 Lawn Avenue, the home of Marion and Cliff Rice, the new drama group was formed. One of the reasons for its inception, was to enable ladies to take part in dramatic productions at the Methodist Church, as the successful Pantomimes were all male cast. They were called the 'Q.T's' because the group had some difficulties at the church with regard to the licensing, the limited seating, safety requirements and the lack of up-to date facilities on the small stage area. Hence the title Q. T's (as in the saying on the Quiet). The first play produced by Marion (Wainwright) was 'Pittybeck', a Yorkshire Mill farce and I was privileged to be in the cast. However the group was, and still is, very successful and large donations continue to be made to worthy causes. The group no longer meets at Birstall, having moved to Syston some years ago and now perform on the stage at the Wreake Valley College Theatre.

On a national note, February 3rd was the date of the severe East Coast Flooding.

On June 2nd we were able to see the Coronation of Queen Elizabeth II on our television screens. It was a very wet day!

1954 The telephone exchange in Johnson Road was becoming overloaded and the National Telephone Company purchased land on Fielding Road and began to make plans for a new exchange that would cater for all the new 'home occupiers' moving into the Jelson Estate on Greengate Lane.

Roger Bannister ran the mile in under 4 minutes on the Iffley Rd. track at Oxford on May 6th.

1955 The long awaited High School at Stonehill was opened with Harold Heaps as Headmaster.

The Lawn Cinema continued to be very well supported and an advert for April this year informed us that, from Monday 4th to Wednesday 6th the main film, in Technicolor, was "Passion" with Cornell Wilde and Yvonne De Carlo. The supporting film, the little one, was "Silver Lode". On Thursday 7th until Saturday 9th, it was Humphrey Bogart and Van Johnson in "The Caine Mutiny", also in Technicolor".

1956 Ernest Marples introduced the Premium Bond scheme on 1st November.

1957 On Friday the 10th February a large earth tremor occurred at 3.43pm, with the epicentre in Charnwood Forest. It severely shook the houses in Birstall.

On the 23rd March the Methodists carried out a stone laying ceremony for their new Church.

The little wooden shop run by the Co-op on Rosetree Avenue closed in May this year and by December a brand new enlarged shop was opened on the same site. Staff employed by the Co-op at the time of the reopening included Edna Chester, Joan Ward, Maisie Slater, Barbara Ashworth, Sid Webb, David Hill and the manager, Mr Beckett.

1958 The new Methodist Church was ready for worship and on the 28th June Mr William (Bill) Sibson performed the Opening ceremony on behalf of his father, Mr Tom Sibson, who was not well at the time. The cost of the whole project amounted to £18,000 of which £5,000 was donated by the J.Arthur Rank Trust. It is important to refer to the fact that the 'Sibson' family have very long connections with the village. The earliest reference is of a 'Sibbesdon' in 1327 or Sytheston' in 1301.

The local British Legion cricket team played one of its last matches on the field at the top of Greengate Lane, before moving to the top part of the School Lane Playing Fields. This year they were in the semi-final of the Midland Area Cup against Southam from Warwickshire.

1959 Sir William Brockington died on the 14th February and was buried in Birstall churchyard alongside his wife Jessie and their daughter Sheila, who had predeceased them in 1940. The original gravestone, set up in 1940 in Birstall Churchyard, has an interesting inscription at the base. Apparently Sheila had been born in the springtime and also died in early March. The inscription reads, "*She came with the snowdrops and she passed away with the snowdrops*".

With the retirement of Mr William Boyer, of Boyer's Buses, the company was sold to 'Midland Red'. They had served the villages along the Soar valley for 48 years. Allen's buses and Kemp & Shaw also ceased trading around this time. Kemp & Shaw had, in the late twenties, taken over the business of 'Eclipse' buses from the Branston family, who had lived at the 'Mill House', at the bottom of Church Hill.

During the 1940's and 50's and before television really 'took off', we were dependant on the radio or wireless for entertainment other than that provided by the local cinemas. During a visit to Bletchley Park near to Milton Keynes in September 2002, I copied a list of popular radio programmes, from the 'museum wireless room' of war time enigma code breaking fame and am sure that some of you will remember them and how we used to listen with great regularity. I have listed these and they can be found in **Appendix II.** — at back before Index

February 1947. Deep snow for weeks. Ernest Green, employed by Ralph Hallam, taking the milk from Cliffe Farm to Johnny Adams on Perseverance Road

1947. Some months later.
The trees are in full leaf and the milk is still being delivered.

1952. Photograph of Birstall Methodist Sunday School taken on the occasion of Ralph Hallam celebrating 21 years as Sunday School Superintendent.

May 1957. The opening of the newly refurbished Co-op on Rosetree Avenue. The happy smiling faces belong to: David Hill, Betty Lawrence, Joan Ward, Mr. Beckett, Maisie Slater, Sid Webb and Edna Chester.

1958 British Legion Cricket Team, photographed in front of the pavilion at the top of Greengate Lane near to where Fieldgate Crescent and Queensgate Drive are now. The semi final of the British Legion Midland Area Cup against Southam. Back row: Ernie Sage, Cedric Stevens, Steve Underhill, Ken Newton, Joe Bradshaw, Terry Stretton, Ivan Hill, and Ken Chester. Front row: Les Brown, Freddie Richards, Alec Davis, John Moore and Bob Bell.

7th October 1966
Tim,Richard and Rachel Kilby off to the "Harvest Festival". The marrow grown by Clarence Truman weighed 28lb. and was 34 inches long.

1986. HRH Prince Charles accompanied by HRH The Princess of Wales visiting the part of Abbeyfield known as Grove House. - P84

1960 - 1969

1960 Longslade Upper School was opened in September. Mr E. A. Finch was the first Headmaster and the school was built to cater for 650 pupils. The initial intake in September was 140 pupils with provision for 300 in September 1961. Besides Birstall, pupils came from the Scraptoft area, Rothley, Mountsorrel and Thurmaston.

The Farthing ceased to be legal tender.

1961 The extensions to the Parish Church were completed this year and the new enlarged premises were opened by Miss Henson. The cost of the alteration was £45,000. The modernised church has a most impressive Tester over the altar table. This was designed by a local girl, Beulah Wright, an ex pupil of Rawlins Grammar School. The inscription around the tester reads, **ECCE AGNUS DEI QUI TOLLIT PECCATA MUNDI**, which translated means 'Behold the Lamb of God which taketh away the sin of the world'.

The Birstall Flower Lovers held their inaugural meeting this year and their first president was Mary Cook.

In November the Birstall Methodist Church formed the First Company of the Girl's Life Brigade. The Rev. Harold Langham was the Chaplain and the first captain of the Company was Mrs Jean Yates.

Mr A. H. G. Heaps, the headmaster of Stonehill Secondary School reports that there are now 640 boys and girls attending the school and each day the school prepares about 500 dinners!

An interesting note in the Leicester Advertiser of the 7th April states that 'Leicester's first parking ticket was issued last Saturday. The unlucky motorist announced his intention to fight the case.'

The population this year had exceeded the 10,000 mark.

1962 On the 24th November the BBC launched the satirical programme 'That was the week that was' (TW3). It was televised on Saturday nights and was hosted by David Frost.

1963 We all felt the impact of the 'Beeching Axe' and Belgrave and Birstall station, along with Rothley and Quorn, closed in March. There had been a general rundown of the line since 1958 when the original express services were replaced with semi-fast trains between Marylebone and Nottingham. George Atkinson, whose widow Eileen lives on Cliffe Road, had been the ticket collector at the Station and after the closure he was given a job as a Shunter in the Fox Street depot of Leicester's London Road Station.

On the 11th July the new Telephone Exchange on Fielding Road was commissioned.

The great train robbery took place on the 8th August and £2.6m in mailbags was stolen.

Where were you on Friday the 22nd November this year when President John F. Kennedy was assassinated in Dallas?

Due to heavy criticism, TW3 was taken off the TV in December.

1964 The 'Greengate' building of Highcliffe School was built this year but because of the overcrowding at Riverside School many children were transferred earlier to the old Telephone exchange in Johnson Road. Highcliffe was opened eventually in 1965. The Infant School, named the 'Elmfield' building', was completed in 1967, when many more children were moved from Riverside. There is still a site problem with water from a spring that is allowed to flow into a storm drain. Previously it ran into a large pond that was in the field, of Cliffe Farm, near to the Greengate Lane building.

1965 Sir Winston Churchill died on the 24th January and was honoured by a State Funeral.

On the 5th October, the old thatched farmhouse and cottage at the top of Church Hill was auctioned. It had been a farmhouse and buildings for many centuries. The last occupants were Tom and Gertie Sibson, and their daughter Margaret. Previous occupiers were Ernest Hallam and family and before that William Sutton and his family. A long way back in time it had been three cottages, and there is still evidence of the other doorways.

The Post Office tower in London was opened on the 7th October.

Housing continued to grow dramatically. Bruce Fletcher constructed the houses on the 'Orchard Estate', north of Lambourne Road. All the avenues on the 'Fletcher' part of the estate were named after Apple trees, except Dalby Avenue, which was named in honour of Ernest Dalby who had been a long time chairman of the Parish Council.

1966 The last few houses to be built in the village, on Riversdale Close, Farm Close and Whiles Lane were built, about this time by Jelson's who also built Henson Close. Apart from any further 'infill' the Parish was now fully developed right up to its boundaries.

Only one sporting entry of consequence this year and that was on the 30th July, England won the world cup at Wembley!

The remaining steam train services on the old great Central line all ceased on the 3rd September with the last special running from London to Manchester.

1967 One tragic piece of development took place this year. Five beautiful cottages on Front Street, known as Paget Cottages were demolished, and replaced with 6 Shops and 6 Maisonettes now called Libra Parade. Most people agree that they are a bit of an eyesore! The old cottages were the original 'Birstall Workhouse' until provision for this facility was made available in Mountsorrel in 1840.

The Wooden School at the Infant School, where the present library is now, was eventually demolished and replaced with temporary accommodation for the Libraries Service.

Kilby's Greengrocer Shop, in the former stables of Birstall Hall, on Roman Road, closed on the 11th November after having traded there from the end of the previous century. The trend in local shopping and the upsurge of the 'Supermarket' meant that many small shops had difficulty in competing with the changes in modern shopping methods.

1969 The population was 12,500.

The last Diesel Sprint Trains ran along the old Great Central Railway line on the 5th May. There had been since

September 1966, a limited service between Nottingham (Arkwright Street) and Rugby (Central), stopping only at East Leake, Loughborough (Central), Leicester (Central), Ashby Magna, and Lutterworth. It was a sad day! Many people remember folk who had, in years past, worked for the railway. Two characters in particular were Walter Veasey and Alf. Chester. They were 'lengthsmen' and for years they had inspected the line, looked after the embankments and checked for all manner of things. Walter looked after the lines from the Abbey Lane sidings to the middle of Bamber's Wood, where at 'Fox Covert' he would meet up and chat with Alf who was responsible for the lines into Rothley and beyond. Note: The point where each ones responsibility ended was about the middle of Bamber's Wood, at appoint half way between the two 'Distance Signals' for Birstall and Rothley and where the road bridge over the new A46 is now situated. Fox Covert was half way through the wood. It is rather sad that tasks of this nature are no longer performed in this manner. Walter Veasey was a member of the Birstall Cricket Club and had married a widow named Mrs Tomlin, who had two sons, Lewin and Cyril. They lived at 33 Front Street. Lewin was a piano teacher and Cyril, was also an accomplished musician. In later life Walter Veasey was for many years, still on duty with the cricket club but always as an Umpire. Alf Chester had worked for the Railway and helped in its construction. He originally lived in Northampton, but when the G. C. Railway reached Rothley, he decided to settle there. Alf was a Methodist Local Preacher and although his delivery was rather 'rural', he was a very popular and much loved character. Other employees of the railway were Mr Cooper, the Station Master, Mr Reynolds, the signalman and later Mr Atkinson, also a signalman and booking clerk.

On a universal note the 26th July was the date that Neil Armstrong stepped on to the surface of the Moon. This was indeed one giant step for mankind.

Birstall Abbeyfield Society came into being when a decision to go ahead with their project to convert a house in Church Hill into old peoples flatlets was taken at a meeting on Tuesday 21st October. The estimate for the work was about £6,000. Originally it was thought that the cost would be around £3,000 to £4,000. The first event to raise money was an open day on the 20th November at 'The Clock House', Roman Road, the home of Mrs Jane Simpson.

1970 - 1979

1970 The Lawn Cinema finally closed its doors on Saturday 17th October. The final programme was 'Carry on up the Jungle', supported by 'Mr Jericho'. The closure surprised everybody, as in the adverts for that week a footnote said, 'Mon. next', Paul Newman in 'Winning'. Unfortunately, those turning up to see Paul Newman on Monday were met by locked doors. This unannounced action caused considerable ill feeling! However, Maisie Slater (nee Walton) tells me that for a long while the takings had been very low. She and her family were not really surprised as on the previous Friday, the evening takings only amounted to £13.00. This was not even enough to pay the staff.

Sadly, it was the onset of television that caused the Cinema to close. There just were not enough customers to warrant the 'Lawn' remaining open. The Lawn Cinema had been a main artery in the village in that practically the whole community used it and had been grateful for the warm and friendly atmosphere that was to be found there in one of the 705 seats. Bert Pollard was the manager and kept that position for the whole of the cinema's existence. Birstall even had its own family of 'The Walton's!' Mrs Mabel Walton was the cashier and her family were also employed there. At one time Mabel was in the cash office, June, her daughter, was looking after the balcony, Maisie, another daughter, was in charge of the stalls and her son Frank (Bud) was the projectionist. Maisie tells me that on the first of the three evenings she watched the film, on the second night she listened to the background music and on the third night she kept an eye on the two rows of double seats at the back of the stalls! If ever anything went wrong and it sometimes did, an S O S was sent out for Bert who could be usually found in one of two places. When the premises were demolished a Supermarket was erected for Mac

Fisheries. One further sad note is that Mrs Walton, who as previously stated, was the cashier for all but the first few years, asked the owners of the Cinema if she could have the chair that she had used in the office for so long. To everybody's regret, this never materialised!

1971 Decimal currency was introduced on the 15th February and the conversion rate meant that a New Penny was worth 2.4 OP and with a former shilling becoming 5 New Pence, it was most confusing, especially for the older generation. When you go shopping now you have to be able to convert ounces to grams. You can do this quite easily if you multiply the ounces by 28.35. I do think that if the good Lord had wanted us to go metric, he would only have chosen Ten Disciples.

The Abbeyfield Society opened its first house in the village, in Regent House on Church Hill only two years after the initial meeting was held to launch the original idea. It was called 'Barnes House' after Betty Barnes who had resided at 'The Cottage' Front Street. Col. Pen H. Lloyd, Chairman of the Leicestershire County Council performed the opening ceremony on the 18th September. The whole project could have been completed much earlier, but for the longevity of a lady (or lovable character) named Emily Measures, who continued to live in an adjoining cottage at 2 Netherhall Lane, until she died.

1972 Penman's built 12 houses on Park House Close, off Curzon Avenue, on land that was previously occupied by one large house called 'Park House'

1973 Mr Norman W Wakefield retired as Headmaster of Riverside Junior School and Mr Trevor Rushby was appointed as his replacement. Mr Rushby had returned to England after a spell of teaching in Germany with the British Forces. Mr Wakefield had been a very successful and popular Head having originally been Senior Master and Acting Head at Roundhill. I personally owe him a great debt of gratitude as throughout the whole of my school career, he more than any other teacher had the greatest influence upon me. He was always a gentleman, for many years after retirement, he would always address me as 'Mr Kilby'. It was whilst at Roundhill that he and his wife, Doris, became married and we scholars collected for a presentation Tea Service. When he retired, I was privileged to be Chairman of the Managers at Riverside and we were pleased to present him with a Woodturning Lathe. In my words of thanks to him on behalf of the school and the Education Authority, I referred to him by his 'nick name' Duggie, as that was what he had been called at Roundhill. Apparently in his early days at Roundhill, there was a popular comedian on the radio called Duggie Wakefield and because of this the name stayed with him.

1974 The Local Government Act on the 1st April saw the demise of the Barrow upon Soar Rural District Council. This was a sad day for many people. From that date we, and all the other 31 villages in the Barrow area, along with Shepshed, joined Loughborough and became part of Charnwood Borough Council.

The New Library was opened on the 5th November 1974.

1976 The new playing fields at the top of Harrowgate Drive were officially opened on the 6th May.

1977 We celebrated the Silver Jubilee of Her Majesty Queen Elizabeth II. There were several exhibitions in the Village and at Wanlip. On reflection, there was very little organised in June 1953 at the time of the Coronation!

Stonehill School came into the Sporting news when their girl's hockey team were reported in the Leicester Mercury to have won every match they had played for three years. This was a remarkable achievement, which had a great deal to do with their coach, Mrs Diana Batterham.

1978 The government introduced 'May Day'.

Charnwood Borough Council built 25 Warden controlled flats at Riversdale Court, for elderly folk, and Miss F M Henson MBE performed the opening ceremony on the 16th November.

1980 - 1989

1981 The Methodist Coffee Shop opened this year, on the 2nd March. It had been a 'dream' of Mrs Nancy Stuart's and for many years has proved to be a very popular meeting place for folk of the Village. Nancy was the wife of Tony and mother of Chris and Janet. Nancy was, many years earlier, the instigator of both the Methodist 'Young Wives' and the 'Mid Wives' which in due course was renamed 'The Thursday Group'

1983 The first edition of the 'Birstall Post' was issued on the 23rd July. This has proved to be an excellent newspaper.

1984 The Birstall and District Local History Society, was formed. The President is John While who resides in Canada.

The Joint Ecclesiastical Parish of Birstall and Wanlip was established.

April saw the opening of the 'Greengate Medical Centre'.

The Parish Council inaugurated a 'Book of Trees' to record the many gifts of trees made to the village. This is kept in the offices of the Council and shows, in beautiful calligraphy, all the names of the donors and where their trees have been planted. Many local groups and societies have over the years made gifts of trees and amongst them are the A T C, the Choral Society, Nat. West and Barclays Banks, The Boys' Brigade, The Scouts and the Guides, The Methodist Ladies' Thursday Group, The Highcliffe Town's Women's Guild, and the Local branch of the Royal Society for the Protection of Birds. Many are given in memory of a loved one.

Col. R.A.St.G. Martin, OBE, JP, LL opened Grove 'House' at Abbeyfield on the 12th June. This was a brand new building adjacent to 'Barnes House'. Fred Grove was present at the ceremony.

1986 There was a visit by The Prince of Wales and Princess Diana. We were all thrilled to witness the arrival on the playing fields of the Prince's red helicopter. The Prince, as President of the Abbeyfield Society, came to visit and view the new part of Abbeyfield, named Grove House in honour of Fred Grove, who had worked hard, not only for the Abbeyfield Association but for the whole Village and the Community. After the ceremony Prince Charles went to another engagement in the Melton area, whilst Diana returned to Highgrove in the helicopter.

The house at 20 Front Street, where Jimmy Lines had run his market garden right up to the date he died in April 1923 was, after the death of his last surviving daughter, Annie, converted into flats. The Lines family were possibly best remembered by the extrovert nature of the three daughters of Jimmy and his wife, Elizabeth. They, contrary to their parents were members of the Socialist Party and were active in the 'Votes for Women Suffragette movement' Of the three daughters, Nancy, (called Annie by her friends) kept house, Eva was a teacher at the National School at Belgrave and a third daughter, Alice, married Jim Muddimer, a bookmaker of Belgrave. The land on the corner of Front St., similar to that of the Church Yard, was built up by soil that had been excavated from the river Soar at the time the canal was created in the late 1790's. In latter years it always grew a good crop of Rhubarb. The new and very desirable flats were given the name 'St. James Court' and the first occupiers took up residence at the end of March this year.

It was on the 26th April that 'The Little Fox Buses', later to be known as the 'Little Foxes', were introduced to Birstall. On the first day alone there was one bus each way every 15 minutes for 13 hours! (104 per day)

1988 In September the Great Central Railway trust, at a cost of £120,000, extended the railway line from Rothley to Birstall. This was nearly 20 years after the last commercial train was run by British Rail, on the former LNER line. The line was originally opened in 1899 and had never, at any time, made a profit. The Train that ran on the 7th September, for the civic reception, was pulled by a J94. Saddle Tank Engine.

The Roman Catholics were able to move from the Wanlip Lane premises to their new Church on Front Street. This move was made possible by a generous donation from Mr Hughie Murphy.

1989 My grandson Christopher Kilby asked that I mention him in these recollections and the best that I can do for him is to say that on the 26th July this year he was born to Richard and Deborah. He is, at least, the eleventh or twelfth generation of male Kilby's all born in Birstall or whose parents lived in the village at the time of their birth.

Christopher Edward son of Richard & Deborah
1989
Richard William son of John & Rosalie
1961
John Arthur son of Lewis & Jessie
1932
Arthur Lewis son of Arthur & Elizabeth
1898
Arthur son of *William & Elizabeth*
1866

William son of Robert & Mary
1835
Robert son of Thomas & Hannah
1805
Thomas son of Thomas (Robert) & Hannah
1780
Robert son of Robert & Elizabeth
1751
Robert son of Thomas & Mary
1720
Thomas Kilby
????
Thomas------------------died
1707

1990 - 1999

1990 The Goscote Hotel was sold by Barry Young and for some time it fell into dereliction.

1991 The Methodist Church Coffee Shop had been given an adverse surveyors report and it was necessary to rebuild that section. The total cost of the project was £230,000 and once again fund raising schemes were prepared. One such effort, that was to prove to be very popular was a 'Village Garden Trail' and the first of these was held in June. In the same year Johnny Green arranged the first of many 'Annual Duck Races' with the entire proceeds going toward LOROS.

The Rt. Hon Michael Heseltine opened the Leicester North Railway Station.

1993 The opening of the Birstall Medical Centre, in Whiles Lane, took place on the 7th August. The Rt. Hon. Stephen Dorrell MP. Secretary of State for Health, performed the opening ceremony.

Sir Roy Griffiths, President of Age Concern, opened the St. James Day Centre in the former Church Hall on the 7th October. This wonderful achievement was mainly due to the endeavours of the vicar of Birstall, the Rev. Charles Bradshaw, who had been successful applying for a lottery grant for the project.

1994 Several artefacts were discovered in Holt Road, to the rear of numbers 27 & 29, and this once again renews the question of whether there was an original Settlement, in this area, in the Saxon times. The artefacts found were gold torques of very considerable value. There is however a school of thought that suggests they may have come from somewhere else in Leicestershire as the land behind these houses had been used for sand extraction and subsequently became a landfill site.

The Coffee Shop and ancillary rooms at the Methodist Church were rebuilt and opened for just over £200,000.

1995 The Goscote Hall became a Residential Home for the elderly.

Charnwood Borough Council rebuilt the Kensit Cottages at the top of Park Road. The previous six cottages had been built in 1922 by Hannah Clarke in memory of John Kensit who was a prominent member of the 'Protestant Truth Society. The new cottages were officially opened on the 7th January and dedicated 'To the Glory of God'. This time they were given the name 'Hannah Clarke Court'.

On the 8th May, 50 years after the end of World War II, there was a re-enactment of the joint service of 1946 held in St. James Parish Church, with The Choral Society again singing 'The Hallelujah Chorus'.

1996 In January the Parish Council Offices moved from 10 Sibson Road to the refurbished Parish Hall, which had been purchased from the Leicester Diocese for £100,000.

1997 On the 22nd January the combined churches of Birstall and Wanlip signed a covenant of commitment promising, among other things, 'Never to do separately, what we can reasonably do together' e.g. Joint Services and Social Activities. The Covenant was signed by the clergy and lay folk of the three denominations.

At the General Election on the 1st May, Stephen Dorrell was re-elected as MP for Birstall and the surrounding area.

In Loughborough, Andrew Reed won the seat for Labour. Andy is a Birstall lad and although living in Quorn, has many Social, Sporting and Family connections with the village. It is the first time since before 1923 that the Village has boasted an MP from within its midst.

We will all remember the death of Diana, Princess of Wales on the 31st August, after that tragic accident in Paris the night before.

1998 On the 31st July the Leicestershire County Council finally closed The Holt. It had been used continually since 1926, as a home for children who were, for a time, in their care.

1999 The centenary of the Great Central Railway was celebrated on the 9th March in the presence of many civic dignitaries.

The old thatched cottages and the builder's yard that used to stand in 'Square Yard' off Front St. were this year replaced with 5 beautiful dwellings, called 'Square Court'. It is a pity that the original name of 'Square Yard' could not have been used for the cul-de-sac containing the five new dwellings and the four terraced cottages.

Appendix I

Wanlip

1938 Wanlip Hall was demolished this year. This was five years after the death of Lady Augusta Palmer, the lady of the Manor, principal landowner and last occupant of the seat. The Hall, which was next to the Church, was built in the 1750's and was later added to. One occupant was Charles Grave Hudson who was made a baronet in 1791. It was on the death of Sir Archdale Palmer that the title went to his younger brother, Sir George Hudson Palmer, a bachelor who died in 1910. The baronetcy then descended to Sir Charles Palmer of Coleford, Gloucester.

There have been stories of people experiencing 'funny feelings' and talking of frightening visits. It may well have been something to do with the death of nineteen year old, Rasselas Morjan, born in Abyssinia, and rescued from slavery, who died at Wanlip Hall on the 25th August 1839. He is buried in Wanlip Churchyard. Perhaps it was his young spirit that was reluctant to leave its earthly home, that had the aversion to strangers and caused them to experience 'goose pimples' and 'hairs on the neck beginning to stand on end'! One wonders where Rasselas was on the 1st August 1834 when slavery was abolished completely throughout all the British Possessions. It is quite possible he was still in area of Wanlip or Rothley when the anti slavery agitators, William Wilberforce and Zachary Macaulay of Rothley, (Father of Thomas Babington Macaulay, 1st Baron), working from Rothley Temple, introduced the Abolition of Slavery Act.

It is possible that Rasselas was of royal blood and that he was a descendant of the Ethiopian Dynasty. There have been claims that he was even descended from the Queen of Sheba's only son by King Solomon, who was named Menelik The Emperor Haile Selassie of Ethiopia (1892-1975) took the name Ras Tafari (Ras is Amharic for Prince). He was a direct descendant of Menelik II. (1844-1913). Haile Selassie was a prominent guest at the coronation of Queen Elizabeth II in 1953. One further fact is that the movement called Rastafarianism has its origins in Ethiopia where the belief was held that Haile Selassie was a 'Divine God'

Once, the Hall was the home of Sir William Pepperell, who served in the North American war of 1745. He was in command of 4,000 militiamen, who in April that year sailed in British ships from Boston against Louisbourg and after seven weeks of attack, the colonials captured the supposedly impregnable fortress there and were able to rescue the British from the ruins of the fort at Canso, Nova Scotia, where the French in 1744 had captured and destroyed the fort. Sir William was awarded a casket that became one of the art treasures of Wanlip Hall. France sent further fleets in 1745 and 1747 but they were never able to recapture Louisbourg. These wars were to be known as 'King Georges Wars.' At the end of the wars in 1748, Louisbourg was returned to the French in exchange for British control of Madras, in India.

By 1933 the new owner of the estate was Mr J E Tomkinson, a brother of Brigadier H Tomkinson, Master of the King's Race Horses, who later became Palmer-Tomkinson. Apparently the Hall at one time held many valuable heirlooms. Several paintings had been exhibited at the Royal Academy. One room had its walls covered in Chinese paper that was 170 years old. Even five years before the hall was demolished there were few signs of the paper fading and the design was cleverly taken round the entire room without repetition. It depicted a Chinese procession. Before the Hall was demolished there was an impressive Banyan tree, in the grounds, which was a kind of Indian Fig Tree with a vast rooting system that threw up many branches.

It was also this year that Wanlip Rectory, which was empty, caught fire and was destroyed. The Leicester Builder F. E. Kirkland purchased the ruined Rectory, which had stood on about four and a half acres. He obtained planning permission to build a considerable number of dwellings but with the onset of the Second World War, these plans were cancelled.

Appendix II

Radio Shows of the 40's and 50's

(This list was taken from the Wireless Room at Bletchley Park)

1 Much Binding in the Marsh. Kenneth Horne, Richard Murdoch, Sam Costa & Maurice Denham.
2 Worker's Playtime. from Munitions Factories.
3 It's That Man Again. Tommy Handley, Jack Train, [Col. Chinstrap], Molly Weir,[Mona Lot]
4 Henry Hall's Guest Night. Henry Hall speaking.
5 Hi! Gang. Ben Lion and Bebe Daniels
6 Garrison Theatre. Jack Warner, Elsie and Doris Waters. [Girt & Daisy]
7 Monday Night at Eight.
8 The Ovalteenies
9 Just William. With Violet Elizabeth Bott.
10 Ack Ack Beer Beer. Arthur Askey and Richard [Stinker] Murdoch
11 Crazy Gang. Nervo Knox, Noughton Gould, Flanagan and Allen.
12 Charlie Chester Show
13 Have a Go. Wilfred Pickles, Violet Carson [piano] Mabel [at the table] & Barney Colohan. [Give em' the money, Barney!]
14 Waterlogged Spa. Eric Barker.
15 Ignorance is Bliss. Harold Berens, Stewart Macphearson & Gladys Hay.
16 Music While You Work. [Munitions Factories]
17 Happidrome. Ramsbottom, Enoch and Me.
18 Stand Easy
19 Merry go Round. Eric Barker
20 Band Wagon. Arthur Askey
21 The Gang Show. Ralph Reader
22 Radio Forfeits. Michael Miles.
23 The Al Read Show
24 Educating Archie. Peter Brough & Archie Andrews.
25 The Clitheroe Kid. Jimmy Clitheroe.
26 Billy Cotton Band Show. Doreen Stevens, Alan Breeze and later, Betty Driver.
27 Dick Barton, Special Agent. Duncan Cars, Snowy & Jock.
28 Paul Temple. [Music: Coronation Scot]
29 The Navy Lark. Eric Barker, Leslie Philips and Jon Pertwee.
30 Take It From Here. Jimmy Edwards, Dick Bentley and June Whitfield. [The Glums
31 Ray's a Laugh. Ted Ray.

32 Life with the Lions. Bebe Daniels and Ben Lion.
33 Opportunity Knocks. Hughie Green.
34 Hancock's Half Hour. Tony Hancock, Sid James, Kenneth Williams & Hattie Jacques.
35 Carol Levis Discoveries.
36 The Goon Show. Harry Seacomb, Peter Sellers, Spike Milligan & Michael Bentene i
37 Round the Horne. Kenneth Horne and Sam Costa.
38 Variety Band Box.
39 PC 49. Brian Reece.
40 The Flying Doctor. Bill Kerr.
41 The Huggetts. Jack Warner, Kathleen Harrison & Petula Clarke.
42 Up the Pole. Jimmy Jewel and Ben Warriss.
43 Journey into Space. Jet Morgan & Jimmy Mutch.
44 Chapel in the Valley. Sandy McPhearson [Mr Drewit]
45 Over the Garden Wall. Norman Evans.
46 Forces Favourites. Ann Shelton, Vera Lynn and later, Cliff Michlemore &Jean Metcalf
47 Very Tasty! Very Sweet!.
48 Record Time
49 In Town Tonight
50 Does the Team Think?

There are still a few more that I can recall!

The Archers, Mrs Dale's Diary, Leslie Welch [memory man], Down Your Way, The Daring Dexters, and Riders of the Range.

Index

Abbeyfield, 78, 80, 84
Acacia Ave. 37
Adler, Miss S A, 20, 41
Agar's Stables, 53
Air Raid Shelters, 49, 51
Air Raid Wardens, 53
Air Training Corp, 58, 83
Allen's Buses, 62, 63, 68
Alpine Gardens, 6
Anderson, John, 49
Andrews, Fish, 42
Archer, Mr, 11
Armstrong, Neil, 78
Ashworth, Barbara, 67
Athow, Miss, 29, 30, 44
Atkins, Fish, 42
Atkinson, George & Eileen, 74, 77
Austin's, (Newsagents), 10
Aylestone Road Gas Works, 4
Bamber's Wood, 31, 77
Bannister, Sir Roger, 66
Barnes & Barnes House, 80
Barrow Upon Soar RDC, 36, 65, 81
Bass, Frank, 54
Bates, 'Guy Harlings', 10
Batterham, D, 82
Battleships, 52
Beadle, William, 10
Beechfield Ave. 27
Belgrave, 4, 5, 28
Belvoir Castle, 30
Bennion, Charles, 5,
Benson, William, 36
Bentleys, Milk Bar, 43
Bird, Sylvia, (Sam), 54
Birstall Choral Society, 60, 83, 88
Birstall & District Local History Soc., 18, 65, 83
Birstall Drama Society, 65
Birstall Flower Lover's Guild, 73
Birstall Golf Club, 5, 11, 44, 54
Birstall Hall, 4, 18, 25, 26, 27, 59, 65
Birstall Hill House, 36
Birstall Jewellers, 42
Birstall Library, 81
Birstall Lighthouse, 7, 62
Birstall Medical Centre, 87
Birstall Mill, 12, 35, 68
Birstall Post, 83
Birstall Rd., 29, 40, 42, 52
Blacksmith's Forge, 13
Blakeway, Evelyn Grace, 4
Blenheim Rd. 65
Bleriot, Louis, 6
Boat House, 10
Boddy, J.A.V. 10
Boer War, 4, 37
Book of Trees, 83
Bouchard Mrs. 42
Bouskell, G. E. 4, 9, 18, 37
Bowler I, 11
Bowman's Butchers, 42
Bowrah, Mr F, 20, 30
Bowrah Miss, Maisie, 30
Boyer's Buses, 62, 68
Bradgate Park, 5
Bradshaw, Rev. Charles, 87
Bramley Rd. 65, 75
Branston, George, 27, 68
Brayshaw, Frank, 38
Briers, F, 10
Briggs E. 'Putty', 10
Bristow T H, 11
British Legion, 41, 52, 67
British Legion, (Women's), 58
Brockington, Sir William, 9, 61, 67, 68
Bryant, Frank, 49
Burley Houses, 34
Burley, John, 34
Burnett, Wilf. 37, 41
Burrell, Miss, 30
Buswell, E, 9, 13
B.U.S.M.C. 5, 10
Butt, Richard, 60

Canal, 5, 26, 33, 84
Cart, Miss, 12
Cartwright, Jim, 11, 44
Cartwright's Shop, 42
Cedar Tree, 26
Cemetery, Greengate Ln. 43, 63
Chamberlain, Rt. Hon Neville PM, 49
Chappell, Dr. 9
Charles, John, 31
Charles, Prince of W, 62, 84
Chester, Alf. 77
Chester, Edna, 54, 67
Church Hall, 12, 39, 65, 87, 88
Churchill, Mrs, 58
Churchill, Sir W, 75
Church Hill, 64, 68, 78, 80
Clarke, Arthur Joseph & George Crisp, 4, 8, 9, 16, 18, 29
Clarke, Hannah, 20, 88
Clarke, Mrs, Inglewood, 10
Clarke, John T. 7, 62
Cliffe Farm, 75
Cliffe Road, 74
Clock House, 8, 78
Coates, A, 35
Coates, W, 12
Cobham, Sir Alan, 44
Cockcroft, G. 38
Colbourn, D, 54
Cole, Bert, 29
Collett, W H, 10
Connell, Rev. R J, 60
Cook, George, Post Office (Sibson Rd), 42
Cook, George, (Roman Rd), 10
Cook, Mary, 73
Coombs, 43
Co-op 5, 11, 30, 43, 67
Copeland Rd., 26
Cottage, The, 6, 26, 39, 80
Coupland, John, 37
Cousins, Gladys, 54
Cricket Ground, 26, 28, 35, 77
Crippen, Dr Hawley Harvey, 7
Crossways The, 27, 43, 56
Cufflin's, 42
Curzon Ave., 25, 27, 28, 29, 31, 32, 36, 59, 80
Curzon, Lord, 25, 28
Daily Mirror, 5
Dakin, Major Jack, 16
Dalby Ave, 75
Dalby, Ernest, 34, 75
Dawes Mrs M, 17, 31
de Bathe, A, 25
Decimal Currency, 80
Diana, Princess of W. 84, 89 +72
Disney, Rev., R B, 6, 13, 20, 29
Dolman, L, 36
Dorrell, Rt.Hon. Stephen M P, 88
Drive The, 4, 18, 26
Duck Race, 87
Duxbury, George, 25
Duxbury, Misses, 11
Earl of Stamford, 52, 58, 64
Earthquake, 67
East Leicester Land Society, 8
East Road, 8
Eclipse Bus, 27, 68
Education Street/Road, 29
Edward VII, 4, 5, 8
Edward VIII, 19, 41
Eiffel Tower, 7
Elizabeth II, 41, 61, 64, 66, 81, 82
Elmfield Ave. 37, 75
Evacuees, 53
Faire Bros., 12
Farm Close, 75
Farmer, Steve, 52
Farrell, Dukes Mr. 11
Fazey, Miss, 20, 44
Fenton, Rev. J H, 49
Fergusson Wm. 10
Fieldgate Crescent, 56
Fielding-Johnson, 9, 14, 18, 19, 26, 27, 28, 36, 64
Fielding Rd, 37, 38, 66, 74
Fire Station, 53
Firfield Ave., 27
Fletcher, Bruce, 75
Foot & Mouth, 27
Forder, Joyce & Fred, 54

Fox, Wm. & Peggy, 40
Freehold Rd. 8
Freeman, Hardy & Willis, 34
Freer, J L, 13
Freestone, Norman, 52
Fresh Approach, 43
Front St., 9, 13, 35, 41, 42, 44, 62, 76, 77, 80, 84, 85, 89
Furburrows, 42
Gallipoli, 35
Gallows, 64, 65
Garden Trail, 87
Garner, F, 28, 32
Gas Masks, 53
George, Lloyd, 6
George V & VI, 8, 41, 60, 64
Gibson, Geoffrey & Fred, 9, 28
Girls Brigade, 73, 83
Goadby Mr, 11
Godfrey's, 12
Gooding, Ald. T, 10
Goscote Hall, 14, 19, 26, 36, 51, 87, 88
Grange The, 34, 52
Greasley's, Bakers, 42
Great Central Railway, 74, 76, 77, 85, 89
Green, F, (Wigston), 13
Green, Jim (Snap), 34
Green, John, 18, 19
Green, Johnnie, 87
Greengate Lane, 28, 30, 43, 53, 55, 63, 66, 67, 75
Gregorian Calendar, 40
Grove, Fred, 84
Gunby, D, 13
Gwendolin Ave., 27
Haines, C, 37
Hall Cottage, 8
Hall Stables, 8
Hallam, Christine, 49
Hallam, Ernest, 75
Hallam, Horace, 28, 44, 54, 56
Hallam, Ralph & Kathleen, 49, 54
Hallam, Ald. R, 10
Hallam, William, 13
Hannah Clarke (Court), 88
Hannah, Sgt. John VC & Janet, 57, 59, 61
Harley St. 7
Harris, C, 13
Harrison, Isaac, 31
Harrowgate Drive, 81
Harrogate Drive. Playing Fields, 81
Hartopps, Off Licence, 42
Hartshorn, H, 10, 27
Head Gardener, 8, 18
Heard, Miss, 5, 10
Henson Close, 76
Henson, Miss F M, 73, 82
Hermitage Road, 65
Higginson, Louis, 60
Highcliffe School, 75
Hill, David, 67
Hill Rise, 27
Hillsborough, 31
Hincks, Harriet, 11
Hirst, T G, 26, 40
Hoggett C, 11
Holly Hayes, 26, 36
Holt Rd. 32, 87
Holt The, 5, 26, 89
Home Guard, 52, 59
Homesteads, 30
Horgan, Father, 58
Hoskins, John, 55
Hunt, Albert, 12, 27, 39
Hunt, Harry, 54
Hunt, C E, (Tempest Rd) 11
Innocent, G W, 4, 9, 27
Iris Ave., 35
Jarvis, W (Bill), 37
Jelson's, 5, 76
Johnson, Miss, 10
Johnson Rd., 9, 26, 32, 37, 43, 60, 66, 75
Joyce, C, 13
Joyce, Mabel, 42
Kedleston Avenue, 28
Kedleston Hall, 25, 28
Kemp and Shaw, 27, 34, 62, 63, 68
Kennedy, J F, 74
Kenney's, Ironmongers, 42
Kenney, Mrs M, 31

Kensit, John (Cottages), 20, 88
Kilby Ave., 25, 55
Kilby's, 8, 16, 17, 25, 33, 76, 81, 85
Kilby, Chris, 85
Kirby Muxloe, 56
Kirk, E, 13
Kingdom, Tommy, 19
Lambourne Rd. 65, 75
Land Army Girls, 54
Land Mine, 55, 56
Lane, Geoff. 42, 55
Langham, Rev. H. 73
Larsen Dr. 11
Laundons, Outfitters, 43
Lawn Avenue, 38, 65
Lawn Cinema, 38, 40, 41, 44, 52, 64, 66, 79, 80
Lawn Lodge, 9
Lawn The, 9, 25, 37, 38, 40
Leicester City F C. 62
Leicester Mercury, 34, 35, 82
Leicester Paper Staining Co. 12
Leicester Royal Infirmary, 52
Legionaries, The, 52
Letts Mr & Mrs, 11
Libra Parade, 76
Lines, Jimmy, 84
Llewellyn, Rev., D E K, 28, 29
Lloyd, Col. P H, 80
Loakes, Ray, 52
Lodge Farm/Fludes Farm, 18, 26
Longslade Sch. 73
LOROS, 41, 43
Loughborough Rd., 20, 36, 37, 38, 53, 61, 62, 65
Lucas, Joyce, 54
Luck, W (Bill), 52
Mackley, R, 11
Mafeking, 37
Major, John, 31
Mansfield J, 26
Martin, Lt. Col. Sir R, & Andrew, 64, 84
Mason Dr. 10
Mayes, Michael, 55
McKenna, J, 36
Meadow Ln. 65
Meadway, The, 27
Measures, Emily, 80
Men's Pantomime, 60, 65
Methodist Church, 28, 31, 33, 49, 53, 60, 61, 65, 67, 73, 83, 87, 88
Michael, David, 55
Midland Railway, 12
Midland Red, 33, 63, 68
Mons, Battle of, 14
Montrose *SS,* 7
Moody's, Ladies/Gents Hairdresser, 42
Moon, The, 78
Morrison, Herbert, 49
Moulson H, 9
Murphy, Hughie, 85
National Children's Home, 61
National Health Service, 62
National School, 13, 20, 29, 39
Netherhall Ln. 37, 54, 80
Newham's, Cycles, 43
Newton, Sydney, 60
Newton's, 'The Pines', 10
New York, 7
Oakfield Ave, 37, 64
Observer Corps, 52
Ogden, Cecil, 8
Old Age Pension, 6
Old Cottage The, 8
Old Elms, The, 40
Orchard Rd. 65, 75
Orton's, Coal Merchants, 11
Painter, Mrs L, 9
Palmer, Joshua, 12
Pallett, J W, 62
Parker, Dr. 11
Parker, Rev. H. 5
Parker, S F, 62
Parkes, John, 37
Park House, 26
Park House Close, 80
Park Rd. 7, 20, 37, 44, 62, 88
Pasch, Edward, 54
Partington, Miss, 9
Patrick's, Butchers, 43
Payne, W (Bill), 52
Pearns, Newsagents, 43

Pepperell, Sir William, 91
Perseverance Rd. 8
Petrol Station, (Bottom of Red Hill), 11
Pickaver, Miss, 20, 30
Playing Fields, 27, 34, 37, 43, 44, 64, 67
Plough Inn, 52
Pole, Walter, 60
Police, 11, 12
Pollard, Bert, 41, 79
Poplar Ave., 56
Population, 4, 20, 33, 64, 74, 76
Pratt, Rev. Francis, 60
Pre-Fabs, 59
Premium Bonds, 67
Priestnall's, 10
Q. T's, 65
Quail, Builder, 37
Radio Programmes, 1940's, 68,
  Appendix II (93)
Radio Transmitter, 7
Rank, J Arthur, 67
Ratcliffe College, 58
Ration Books, 54
Rats, 34
Rawlins Grammar School, 73
Reading Room, 29, 31, 58
Red Hill, 4, 20, 36, 64
Reed, Andrew, M P, 89
Reed, Sgt. James, 14, 16
Retreat, The, 27
Reynolds, Mr, 77
Rice, Marion & Cliff, 65
Richardson, Mr. 11
Riley, Dot, 54
Riversdale Court, 82
Riverside Close, 75
Riverside Sch. 33, 39, 44, 51, 53, 57, 58,
  60, 75, 76, 80
River Soar, 4, 26, 84
Road Blocks, 28
Roman Rd. 8, 9, 16, 18, 31, 36, 55, 65,
  76, 78
Rookery, The, 17, 37
Rosetree Ave., 67
Rosminians, 58
Rothley, 7, 74, 77, 85
Roundhill Sch. 33, 53, 61, 81
Rudkin, G H, 10
Rushby, Trevor, 80, 81
Russell, A, 11
Rutland Street, 34
St. George's Church, 9
St. James's Church, 4, 20, 28, 33, 37, 38,
  40, 41, 43, 60, 68, 73, 83, 84, 87, 88
St. James' Court, 84
St. James' Day Centre, 87
St. Theresa's Church, 42, 58, 85, 88
Sarson, Jim, 52
Saxon Beast, 33
School Lane, 6, 18, 28, 31, 35, 37, 64
Scott, Shirley, 28, 60
Scout Hut, 5, 83
Shar, Dentists, 42
Shaw, Tom, 62
Sherriff, Amos, 30
Sibson, Ernest, 35
Sibson Rd., 27, 29, 42, 56, 88
Sibson, Tom & Gertie, 33, 67, 75
Sibson, W (Bill), 67
Simpson, Jane, 78
Sketchley's, 42
Slater, Harry, 32, 36, 38, 42, 60, 65
Slater, June, 60
Sleath, Fred, 52
Slopes, The, 8
Smith, Bert (Blacksmith), 44
Smith, W Fred B, 37, 38
Smith, Mike, 3
Smith, L E, 30, 33, 39
Smith, L O. 9
Social Club, 38, 40, 51, 54, 59
Society Rd. 7
Somerfield, 16
Somme, Battle of, 14, 16,
South Africa, 4
Spiers, E, 12
Spradbury, Mr. 5
Spitfires, 28 52
Square Court, 89
Stacey, J C W, 37, 38
Station Rd., 9, 20
Stone Philip, 11, 42, 56

Stonehill Ave., 37, 38, 56, 61
Stonehill High School, 66, 73, 82
Stuart, Nancy, 83
Supacare, 43
Sutton Annie, Frank & Janet, 64, 65
Sutton, W & Roy, 64
Swann, Mrs, 42
Syston, 9, 19
Taylor, Mark, 40
Taylor's, Sweets, 42
Telephone Exchange, 9, 43, 66, 74
Tempest Bouskell, 34, 37
Tempest Rd. 34, 36
Tester, 73
Thomson, Grocer, 11
Thornton, Rev. R G, 28, 37
Thurmaston Police, 11
Timlocks, 58
Timmis, Chris, 35
Tipping, Mrs, 56
Tollemache Ave., 55
Tomlin, Mrs, Lewin & Cyril, 77
Tomorrow's World Travel, 43
Toone, K K, Greengrocers, 42, 54
Toone Mr. 8
Trams, 5
Triangle, 38, 64
Turner, N, 38
TW3, 74
Veasey, Walter, 77
Vicarage, 11
Victoria, Queen, 4, 30
Victoria Cottages, 6, 31
Vincent, J. C, 11
Vineries, 8
Vladivostok, 19
Wadd, Jack, 8
Wainwright, Mr (Rothley), 7
Wakefield, N W & Doris, 58, 80, 81
Walker, Rev. F W, 28, 29, 37
Walker Rd. 36
Walker, William Henry, 5, 26
Walton's The, 67, 79, 80
Wanlip, 35, 57, 82, 90
Wanlip Ave., 27, 29, 43
Wanlip Hall, 44, & Appendix I (90)
Wanlip Lane, 15, 16, 27, 28, 29, 31, 32, 33, 38, 44, 51, 52, 53, 54, 58, 59, 65
Wanlip Rectory, 44, 92
Ward, Joan, 67
Wardle, Jim, & John, 17, 25, 29, 41
War Memorial, 16, 20
Washington, George, 40
Waterhouse-Reynolds, 26
Wayne Way, The, 27, 42
Webb, Syd, 67 Sid
Wells, W, 15, 35
Went, Rev. James & Miss, 9, 11, 18, 19, 23 27, 28, 37, 39, 40
Went Rd. 37, 62
While, Miss E, & John, 4, 83
Whiles Lane, 40, 42, 62, 75, 87
White Horse Inn, 13, 28
White Horse Ln. 13, 33
Wilkes, G, 12
Wilkinson, S W, 11, 37
Windmill Ave., 37, 52
Wintertons, Grocers, 11, 43
Wolsey Ltd., 32
Women's Bright Hour, 29, 60
Women's Institute, 18
Wood, Alfred, 18
Wood, Sir Edward, 12
Woofenden, W, 13
World War I, 7, 14, 58
World War II, 40, 49, 60, 88
Worthington's, Grocers, 42
Worthington T, 9
Wright, Beaulah, 73
Wright, E, 10
Yates, Francis, 54
Yates, Jean, 73